The Homerton LOGO Manual

Hilary Shuard and Fred Daly

CAMBRIDGE UNIVERSITY PRESS
Cambridge
New York   New Rochelle
Melbourne   Sydney

Published by the Press Syndicate of the University of Cambridge
The Pitt Building, Trumpington Street, Cambridge CB2 1RP
32 East 57th Street, New York, NY 10022, USA
10 Stamford Road, Oakleigh, Melbourne 3166, Australia

© Hilary Shuard and Fred Daly 1987

First published 1987

Printed in Great Britain at the University Press, Cambridge

British Library cataloguing in publication data
Shuard, Hilary
The Homerton LOGO manual.
1. LOGO (Computer program language)
I. Title II. Daly, Fred
005.2'6   QA76.73.L63

ISBN 0 521 33723 2

Contents

Introduction

1 Using LOGO for drawing pictures   1
  1.1 Some primitive commands   1
  1.2 Lowering the pen   2
  1.3 Typing errors   2
  1.4 Abbreviations   2
  1.5 Projects   3

2 REPEAT   4
  2.1 Squares   4
  2.2 Project   5
  2.3 Repeats   5
  2.4 Inputs   5
  2.5 Projects   6
  2.6 Wraparound   6
  2.7 Project   6

3 Procedures   7
  3.1 Teaching the computer   7
  3.2 Extending LOGO's vocabulary   7
  3.3 Making LOGO remember   8
  3.4 Procedures   8
  3.5 Saving your procedures on disk   8
  3.6 Saving your procedures on tape   9
  3.7 Projects   10

4 Editing   11
  4.1 Editing your procedures   11
  4.2 Steering the cursor   11
  4.3 Changing the text   11
  4.4 Editing another procedure   12
  4.5 The function keys   12
  4.6 Erasing   13
  4.7 Project   13

5 The graphics screen and the text screen   14
  5.1 Hiding the Turtle   14
  5.2 Screen modes   14
  5.3 Your workspace   14
  5.4 BBC screen modes   15
  5.5 Changing colours   17
  5.6 Changing modes without SAVE   17
  5.7 Projects   17
  5.8 Stopping the procedure   18

6 Recursion   19
  6.1 What recursion does   19
  6.2 What recursion really does   19
  6.3 Projects   20

7	**Polygons, stars and circles**	**21**
	7.1 Using recursion	21
	7.2 Project	21
	7.3 Heading	21
	7.4 Project	21
	7.5 The Turtle Total Trip Theorem	21
	7.6 Circles	22
	7.7 Projects	22
	7.8 Drawing a circle with given radius	22
	7.9 Projects	24
8	**Variables**	**25**
	8.1 Varying the size of a drawing	25
	8.2 Project	25
	8.3 Procedures that take inputs	26
	8.4 Project	26
	8.5 Colons and quotes	26
	8.6 Local variables	28
	8.7 Coordinates	28
	8.8 Heading	30
	8.9 Projects	30
9	**MAKE and arithmetic**	**31**
	9.1 MAKE	31
	9.2 Project	32
	9.3 Arithmetic	32
	9.4 PRINT	33
	9.5 Variables in arithmetical procedures	33
	9.6 Projects	34
10	**More commands using numbers**	**36**
	10.1 RANDOM	36
	10.2 Other arithmetical commands	36
	10.3 Integer division	37
	10.4 Prefix arithmetic	37
	10.5 Projects	38
	10.6 IF – and tests	38
11	**Words and lists**	**40**
	11.1 A larger project	40
	11.2 Input from the keyboard	40
	11.3 Lists	41
	11.4 Words	42
	11.5 Project	43
	11.6 Variables and their values	43
	11.7 Projects	44
	11.8 Laying out text on the screen	45
	11.9 Projects	46
12	**Tearing lists apart**	**47**
	12.1 Further development of YOUNGLOGO	47
	12.2 Tearing lists apart	47
	12.3 FIRST and BF	48
	12.4 Project	49
	12.5 Other commands which manipulate lists	49
	12.6 Commands which take brackets	50

13	**Single key input**	51
	13.1 RC	51
	13.2 ASCII codes	52
	13.3 Project	53
	13.4 KEY?	53
	13.5 Project	53
14	**Boolean primitives**	54
	14.1 The primitive NOT	54
	14.2 AND and OR	54
	14.3 Commands which use TRUE or FALSE	55
	14.4 Building your own tests	56
	14.5 Projects	57
15	**More about variables**	58
	15.1 Polygons with recursion with variables	58
	15.2 Polyspirals	58
	15.3 Projects	58
	15.4 Local variables	59
	15.5 Levels	61
	15.6 Changing colours	63
	15.7 Project	64
16	**Building up lists**	65
	16.1 A random sentence generator	65
	16.2 LPUT and FPUT	66
	16.3 Choosing a random member of a list	66
	16.4 Making the random sentence	67
	16.5 Projects	68
17	**More about recursion**	69
	17.1 Drawing a tree	69
	17.2 Variations on TREE	71
	17.3 Snowflake curves	71
	17.4 Project	74
18	**List of LOGO primitives**	75
	Glossary	78

Introduction

This manual is intended to give beginners a knowledge of those features of LOGO which are needed to use it in a satisfying way. It takes the reader through LOGO in a structured order, so as to give confidence that major features of the language have been mastered. It is also intended to provide a simpler and more easily understandable introduction to LOGO than do many other books. It has been 'field tested' by many beginners who have attended courses at Homerton College, Cambridge. They have told us when they did not understand what we wrote, and we have tried to improve the explanations.

The intention of Seymour Papert, the developer of LOGO, was to provide a rich environment for children to explore; this environment was intended to lead to a knowledge of computer programming, but also to provide fascination for the beginner. Some readers of this book will be teachers, who are working through LOGO in preparation for using it with children. It is not suggested that children should be introduced to LOGO in the structured way used in this manual. A much more exploratory approach, in which children are encouraged to set and solve their own problems, is recommended. However, from time to time the teacher may need to introduce a new feature of LOGO, so that children can find less laborious ways of tackling projects.

Other readers will be learning LOGO for fun, or for a satisfying introduction to the power of computer programming. Whoever you are, we hope you will have fun as you explore LOGO.

The dialect of LOGO which is used in this book is the LCSI version for the BBC microcomputer. However, you will still be able to use the book if you have another computer and another dialect of LOGO. There is a glossary at the back which gives the equivalent commands in other popular dialects, and you will quickly get used to the changes. You should also refer to the manual which was provided with your own version of LOGO. However, the basic structure of LOGO remains the same in all dialects.

1 Using LOGO for drawing pictures

1.1 Some primitive commands

The LOGO computer language can program the computer to do many tasks. Young children start by using LOGO to make the computer draw pictures. Adults can use LOGO to program the computer to carry out complex tasks, just as they might use another computer language such as BASIC or PASCAL.

Power up the computer and enter LOGO by typing:

>   *LOGO

You will find that the computer already understands a few words of English. You can use these words to tell the computer how to draw pictures.

>   Type CS and press (RETURN).

CS stands for ClearScreen. You should now have a clear screen with an arrow sitting in the middle, pointing towards the top of the screen. This arrow is called the Screen Turtle (or Turtle for short). You are now ready to command the Turtle (which carries a pen with it) to draw on the screen. The computer understands the following commands, and can instruct the Turtle to obey them:

>   FORWARD
>   BACK
>   RIGHT
>   LEFT

However, *each command must be followed by a number*. Type

>   FORWARD   100   (RETURN)

Experiment with some commands – make the Turtle draw some pictures. Each command must end with (RETURN). To clear the screen and start again, use CS. You can also use HOME, to send the Turtle back to its starting position, and CLEAN, which cleans the screen without moving the Turtle.

The Screen Turtle is the little arrow which does the drawing. It is an abstract screen version of the 'Floor Turtle'. The Floor Turtle is a small computer controlled robot invented by Seymour Papert. It carries a felt-tipped pen, and it understands the LOGO language. It draws pictures on paper on the floor, just as the Screen Turtle draws pictures on the computer screen. Young children feel more comfortable with the Floor Turtle. The Floor Turtle and the Screen Turtle do the same things, except that the computer screen is a picture of the floor seen from above. Young children find it more difficult to decide which directions are RIGHT and LEFT on the screen; on the floor they can stand behind the Turtle to help them to decide which way to turn.

Children as young as four or five years old can use the Floor Turtle to make drawings, using only the initial letters F, B, R, L to command the Turtle. (These one-key-press abbreviations are found on some Turtle graphics programs, but are not available on BBC LOGO; however, see para. 1.5 and later chapters of this manual).

1.2 Lowering the pen

You will need to use the commands

      PU   (which stands for *PenUp*)

and   PD   (which stands for *PenDown*)

The effect of these when drawing on the screen is exactly as it would be if the Floor Turtle were using them on the floor. PU lifts the pen, and enables the Turtle to move without drawing a line; PD lowers the pen to enable the Turtle to draw again.

1.3 Typing errors

Press the DELETE key to rub out the last character you typed.

1.4 Abbreviations

It is tiresome, particularly for non-typists, to have to type in the complete command every time, and so most versions of LOGO allow abbreviations. In BBC LOGO the abbreviations are:

FD	FORWARD
BK	BACK
RT	RIGHT
LT	LEFT

The following are also abbreviations, but BBC LOGO will not accept the complete word:

PU	stands for PenUp
PD	stands for PenDown
CS	stands for ClearScreen

Try   FD 60
         RT 90
         FD 60

1.5 Projects

1. Draw some pictures. Enjoy yourself and do not rush this stage; the LOGO environment is designed to enable children to engage in free exploration. Through this exploration they 'learn without teaching'. You need to have the same experience, so that you can see the possibilities.

2. Draw a square, an equilateral triangle, a regular hexagon.

2 REPEAT

2.1 Squares

When you drew a square, you probably did something like this:

```
FORWARD  100
RIGHT    90
FORWARD  100
RIGHT    90
FORWARD  100
RIGHT    90
FORWARD  100
RIGHT    90
```

Notice these points:

(i) You may have omitted the last RIGHT 90; its only purpose is to finish the square *with the Turtle facing the way it started*. This is a good idea for more complicated geometrical drawings; if you finish geometric drawings facing the way you started, then the drawings will combine more easily.

(ii) Your square may have turned LEFT rather than RIGHT, but in either case the *turning number* was 90. Turning numbers are measured in degrees. Even children who do not know about degrees can probably find out for themselves that a turning number of 180 makes the Turtle face the opposite direction, and that a turning number of 90 produces a right angled turn.

The Turtle steers the same way as a person; it measures its turn starting from the direction it is facing.

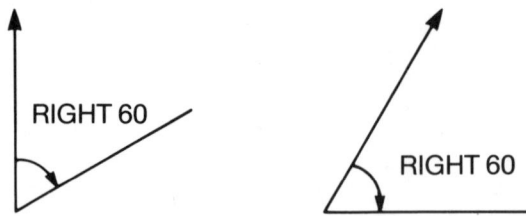

This makes it possible for children to Play Turtle, steering one another by giving Turtle directions. A child who cannot decide how to draw something can often act out, or 'walk through' what is intended.

(iii) The FORWARD number in drawing a square gives the side of the square, measured in Turtle Steps. A Turtle Step is very small.

2.2 Project

Measure the screen in Turtle steps. How tall and how wide is it?

2.3 Repeats

In drawing a square, you typed

    FORWARD   100
    RIGHT 90

four times. To avoid this, you can use the REPEAT command. These commands draw the square:

    REPEAT 4 [FORWARD 100 RIGHT 90]

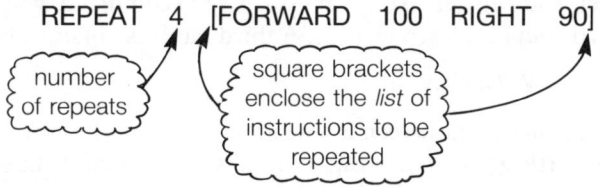

2.4 Inputs

Different commands require different numbers of inputs. The command

    CS

has nothing following it; it has *no inputs*. The command

    FORWARD

needs one number following it, so you have to write something like:

    FORWARD 100

Thus, FORWARD has *one input*, which must be a number.
The command

    REPEAT

takes *two inputs*. The first input is a *number*, telling the number of repeats. The second input is a *list*, the list of instructions which are to be repeated.

In LOGO, lists are always enclosed in *square brackets*. Lists form an important part of LOGO, and are much used in the non-graphics part of LOGO. The list which was used as an input to REPEAT was the list of instructions:

    [FORWARD 100 RIGHT 90]

2.5 Projects

1. Use REPEAT to draw a square, an equilateral triangle, a regular hexagon.
2. Draw some more regular polygons.

2.6 Wraparound

When the drawing gets too big for the screen, the Turtle comes back opposite where it went off. It is like going round the world, but drawing the journey on a map of the world. If you don't like this effect, you can change it by the command

    FENCE

Then you will get an error message if the command would take the Turtle out of the screen area. A third mode is obtained by the command

    WINDOW

In this mode, the screen is a window on a boundless drawing surface; the Turtle goes on drawing when it is off the screen, but we can no longer see it. To get back to the wraparound mode, use the command

    WRAP

2.7 Project

Draw some regular polygons with a great many sides.

3 Procedures

3.1 Teaching the computer

When you enter LOGO, it already understands a few commands, such as FORWARD, CS and REPEAT. It always remembers these commands, which are called LOGO *primitives*. Whenever you ask it to carry out a combination of these commands, such as

>   REPEAT   3   [FORWARD   100   RIGHT   120]

it draws what you ask, and immediately forgets the sequence of commands you gave it.

However, one of the most powerful features of LOGO is its ability to *learn* and remember new commands. To teach LOGO a new command, you have to define that command by telling LOGO how to do it (using what it already knows).

3.2 Extending LOGO's vocabulary

We shall teach LOGO how to do SQUARE. A definition starts with the word TO.

Type

>   TO   SQUARE

The 'prompt' at the beginning of the line changes to >, and LOGO is ready to learn the definition of SQUARE. Type it in:

>   REPEAT   4   [FORWARD   100   RIGHT   90]

When you have finished the definition, type END, but pause for a moment before pressing RETURN.

The screen will now look like that below:

>   TO   SQUARE
>   \> REPEAT   4   [FORWARD   100   RIGHT   90]
>   \> END

The > prompt at the beginning of each line shows that you are making a definition. Some beginners are puzzled by this; they expect the Turtle to draw at once when they type in the commands. What you are doing now is rather like writing the commands down on paper before drawing the picture.

3.3 Making LOGO remember

LOGO automatically remembers SQUARE when you press RETURN after END. There is a very short pause while LOGO stores the *procedure* for SQUARE in its memory; when it has finished, it tells you that it knows SQUARE. When you have taught LOGO the procedure for SQUARE, you can type the command

    SQUARE

and LOGO will draw the whole square, starting wherever the Turtle is.

In the next chapter, you will find out how to EDIT a procedure which has a *bug* in it, and does not do what you want it to do. For the moment, you can get rid of the buggy procedure by typing

    ERASE "SQUARE

The command ERASE (abbr. ER) deletes the named procedure from the computer's memory. Do not omit the quotation mark from "SQUARE; LOGO will complain if you do. A quotation mark is a signal to LOGO that what is coming is a *name*; you are asking LOGO to erase the procedure whose *name* follows.

3.4 Procedures

You can teach LOGO as many procedures as you like, and it will remember them all. Its language grows under your control. The pattern is:

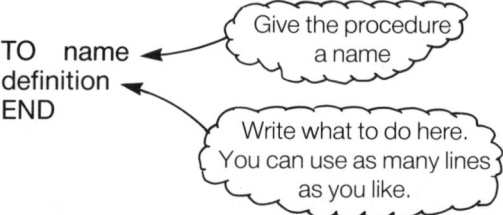

Insert your own material instead of 'name' and 'definition' in the above pattern. We are using the convention that commands are written in capital letters. If lower-case letters are used in a command, this is to tell you to use your own words instead of the words in lower-case.

3.5 Saving your procedures on disk

LOGO will remember your procedures until you turn the computer off. If you want to keep them, you should SAVE them on tape or disk.

To save procedures on *disk*, all you have to do is to type

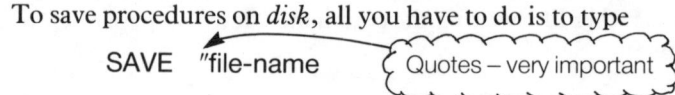

You can use any file-name for the *set* of procedures you are saving. This command saves all your procedures. To get your procedures back at the beginning of the next session, use

>   LOAD   "file-name

If you do not want to save all your procedures, you can write a list of the procedures you want saved; this list goes after the file-name. For example, if you have taught LOGO the procedures SQUARE, TRIANGLE and RUBBISH, and you only want to save the first two, using the file-name JANE, then type

>   SAVE   "JANE   [SQUARE   TRIANGLE]

A single procedure can be saved by using the file-name and the procedure name:

>   SAVE   "JANE   "HOUSE

However many procedures you have SAVEd under the file-name "JANE, the command

>   LOAD   "JANE

brings them all back automatically.

3.6 Saving your procedures on tape

Saving your procedures on tape is not quite so simple. First, you have to tell the computer that you want to use tape, by typing

>   *TAPE

Unfortunately, the computer then stops understanding the command SAVE, and you have to build a procedure to tell it how to save on tape. Type in the procedure SSAVE given below *exactly as it is written*:

```
TO  SSAVE  :FILENAME
(*SPOOL  :FILENAME)  POALL  (*SPOOL)
END
```

Now type

>   SSAVE   "file-name   *Quotes – very important*

to run the procedure you have just built. As you get more used to using LOGO, you will come to see why this procedure works.

You can use any name for the *set* of procedures you are saving. This command saves *all* your procedures. To get your procedures back at the beginning of the next session, use

>   LOAD   "file-name

9

If you do not want to save all your procedures, you can type in another procedure SSSAVE, which is given below:

```
TO  SSSAVE  :FILENAME  :PROCNAMES
(*SPOOL  :FILENAME) PO :PROCNAMES
  (*SPOOL)
END
```

For example, if you have taught LOGO the procedures SQUARE, TRIANGLE and RUBBISH, and you only want to save the first two, using the file-name JANE, then type

```
SSSAVE  "JANE  [SQUARE  TRIANGLE]
```

A single procedure can be saved by using the file-name and the procedure name:

```
SSSAVE  "JANE  "HOUSE
```

However many procedures you have SAVEd under the file-name "JANE, the command

```
LOAD  "JANE
```

brings them all back automatically.

3.7 Projects

1. Teach LOGO the procedures SQUARE, TRIANGLE, HEXAGON.
2. Draw a HOUSE. Draw a STREET of houses.
3. Draw anything you like.

4 Editing

4.1 Editing your procedures

You often want to change a procedure when you have seen what it does. The LOGO *Editor* makes this very easy.

Define a procedure, then type

    EDIT   "procedure-name   (abbr. ED)

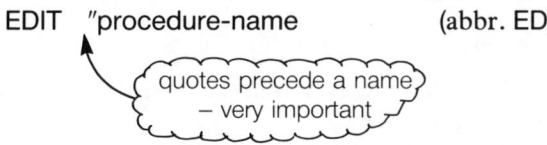
quotes precede a name – very important

You are now in the *Editor*, and you can change the text on the screen.

4.2 Steering the cursor

The four arrow keys steer the cursor round the text.

    ←   moves it to the left,
    →   moves it to the right,
    ↓   moves it down one line,
    ↑   moves it up one line.

Practise steering the cursor around your text.

4.3 Changing the text

To *erase* a character, move the cursor to the character *after the one you want to erase*, and press the DELETE key.

To insert characters into your text, move the cursor to the *exact* position where you want the new characters, and type them in. Notice that everything else moves over to make room for them, and nothing is lost.

Sometimes you need to insert a new line of text. You can type it in at the appropriate place, and let the next line move over, or you can create an empty line by moving the cursor to where you want the line, and pressing RETURN.

When you have finished editing, come out of the edit mode by using CONTROL-C (hold down the CONTROL key and type C). This automatically stores the changes in memory. Use ESCAPE to come out of the edit mode if you do not want to keep any changes you have made.

4.4 Editing another procedure

To edit a different procedure, type

    EDIT   "procedure-name

It is often convenient to use EDIT to write a *new* procedure. Type EDIT "STAR – assuming that you do not have a procedure called STAR in memory. This gets you into the Editor with the screen as follows:

    TO   STAR
    END

Now you can both write and edit the procedure

    STAR

You can edit several procedures at the same time by typing a list of the procedures you want to edit:

    EDIT   [STAR   POLYGON]

No quotes are needed when you write a *list* of procedures to be edited. You can even edit all your procedures at the same time by typing

    EDALL   (stands for *EDitALL*)

4.5 The function keys

The red function keys on the BBC Micro control some operations of the LOGO Editor, and can be used to help with editing.

Some of the more useful keys are:

- F0   erases the character *at the cursor position*
- F1   erases from the cursor position *to the end of line*, but keeps the erased characters invisibly saved ready for you to insert elsewhere.
- F2   inserts text erased by F1 at the cursor position.
- F6   moves the cursor to the beginning of the editor.
- F7   moves the cursor to the end of the Editor.

The key F9 has a particularly ingenious function. It is a *global find and replace*. It asks what to search for, and what to replace it by, and then does the replacement automatically. Start with the cursor at the beginning of the procedure, as F9 searches forward from the cursor position. If there is more than one instance to be found, press COPY F9 to find the next instance.

You will gradually learn to use these keys as you do more editing. You may want to make a label strip for the top of the keyboard, to help you to remember them. A complete list of what all the function keys do can be found on page 130 of the *Logotron LOGO Manual*.

4.6 Erasing

If you are certain you will never need a procedure again, you can erase it from the workspace by using

> ERASE "procedure-name   (abbr. ER name)

Several procedures can be erased at the same time by typing a *list* of them:

> ERASE   [SQUARE   TRIANGLE]

Again, no quotes should be used inside the list.

You can start again with a totally empty workspace by using

> ERALL   (stands for ERaseALL)

This also enables you to follow someone else without switching off the computer.

4.7 Project

Draw some stars. Try this:

```
TO   STAR
REPEAT  8  [FORWARD  80  RIGHT  135]
END
```

Change the angle and see what happens. You may need to change the number of repeats as well.

Some stars turn out to be polygons. Find some. Draw a regular pentagon. Draw a five-pointed star.

How far has the Turtle turned when it has finished drawing a polygon? How far has it turned when it has finished drawing a star? Look for patterns.

The Turtle has drawn a *closed path* when it is back at the same spot facing the same direction as when it started. What can you say about the *total turn* in a closed path?

5 The graphics screen and the text screen

5.1 Hiding the Turtle

The Turtle is very helpful when you are working out how to draw a picture, but it may seem a blemish on the finished work of art. The command

    HT   (stands for *HideTurtle*)

makes it invisible; it is still there, and it draws faster when it is invisible. To make it visible again, use

    ST   (stands for *ShowTurtle*)

5.2 Screen modes

LOGO has two modes of display, a *graphics mode* and a *text mode*. When you first load LOGO, the screen is in text mode, and the whole of it is available for text. When you type a drawing command, the screen goes into graphics mode and displays the drawing screen; six lines of text can be used at the bottom of the drawing screen. When you type a seventh line of text, the top line scrolls up out of sight. You can remove the text from below the drawing by using

    CT   (stands for *ClearText*)

You may want to use CT when your drawing is completed.

Sometimes you want to see a lot of text at the same time. The command

    TS   (stands for *TextScreen*)

moves LOGO into text mode. In text mode, you can clear the screen with CT. To get back to graphics mode, use CS.

5.3 Your workspace

When you have been working for a little time, you will have taught the computer several procedures, such as

    HOUSE
    SQUARE
    TRIANGLE

Your procedures are stored in an area of the computer's memory called the *workspace*. You can see the definitions of all your procedures by using

      POALL   (stands for PrintOutALL)

You will need to move into text mode first, so as to see the complete list of definitions.

If you only want to see the titles of your procedures, you can use the BBC LOGO primitive procedure

      OPPS   (stands for OutPutProcedureS)

Unfortunately, this procedure *outputs* instead of *printing*. You will make more use of outputs later. To make the procedure print, type

      PRINT OPPS

and you will get a list of the titles of all your procedures.

When you save your procedures on tape or disk, the command SAVEALL "file-name saves *everything in the workspace*, so you can start again next time exactly where you were at the end of the last session.

5.4 BBC screen modes

The BBC Micro has eight screen modes of its own, which allow different ranges of colours and sizes of printing. These modes are numbered from 0 to 7. When you enter LOGO you are in Mode 4, which is a black and white mode. Modes 3, 6 and 7 are for text only, but Modes 0, 1, 2, 4 and 5 can be used for Turtle graphics. The computer has a limited amount of memory, and a lot of memory is taken up by colour and the *high resolution graphics* which enable the Turtle to draw thin lines; this leaves less memory space available for the user's procedures. The different modes represent different ways of sharing out memory between:

      very high/high/medium resolution graphics
      a range of colours
      memory available to the user

Mode 4, the mode you are in when you enter LOGO, has:
      high resolution graphics
      black and white only
      plenty of user memory to store your procedures

Full details of the modes are given in the *Logotron LOGO Manual* (p. 98) and the *BBC Micro User Guide* (p. 160). Here, we shall merely start you off on changing modes and introducing colour into your drawings.

Apart from Mode 4, the most useful modes for Turtle graphics are *Mode 1* and *Mode 2*. Their details are:

Mode 1: high resolution graphics

four colours, numbered
- 0 black
- 1 red
- 2 yellow
- 3 white

only a fairly small amount of user memory

Mode 2: medium resolution graphics

sixteen colours, numbered
- 0 black
- 1 red
- 2 green
- 3 yellow
- 4 blue
- 5 magenta
- 6 cyan
- 7 white
- 8 flashing black/white
- 9 flashing red/cyan
- 10 flashing green/magenta
- 11 flashing yellow/blue
- 12 flashing blue/yellow
- 13 flashing magenta/green
- 14 flashing cyan/red
- 15 flashing white/black

only a fairly small amount of user memory

You change mode by typing

SETMODE   number    Insert your own number

You can find out which mode you are in by typing

PRINT   MODE

The computer responds with the number of the mode you are in.

Unfortunately, changing modes may destroy anything which is in the user memory, and LOGO will not always let you change mode until you have erased everything from your workspace. If you get the error message

LOGO   NOT   FRESH

then save your workspace on disk or tape, use ERALL to empty the workspace, change modes, and LOAD the workspace back after the change. Experiment with changing modes.

5.5 Changing colours

You change the pen colour with

>   SETPC   number   (stands for SETPenColour)

The effect varies according to the mode you are in:

>   in *Mode 1*, SETPC 2 produces *yellow*
>   in *Mode 2*, SETPC 2 produces *green*

The background colour can be changed in the same way by using

>   SETBG   number   (stands for SETBackGround)

5.6 Changing modes without SAVE

There is a method of changing modes without saving your procedures on disk or tape. This is based on the fact that the LOGO Editor has some memory of its own. This memory, called the *Edit Buffer*, holds your procedures while you are editing them, and can hold them while you change mode. Carry out the following sequence of commands:

EDALL	stores all your procedures in the Edit Buffer
Press *ESCAPE*	comes out of the Editor, leaving your procedures stored in the Edit Buffer
ERALL	erases your procedures from the workspace, but not from the Edit Buffer
SETMODE number	changes mode
ED	gets you back into the Editor – your procedures are still there
CTRL-C	reads your procedures back into the workspace

5.7 Projects

1. Draw some windmills. Try this:

   ```
   TO   SQUAREMILL
   REPEAT   8   [SQUARE   RIGHT   45]
   END
   ```

   Try some variations, using some of your other procedures.

2. Draw anything you like.

5.8 Stopping the procedure

If anything goes wrong, and you need to stop a procedure while it is executing, use

ESCAPE

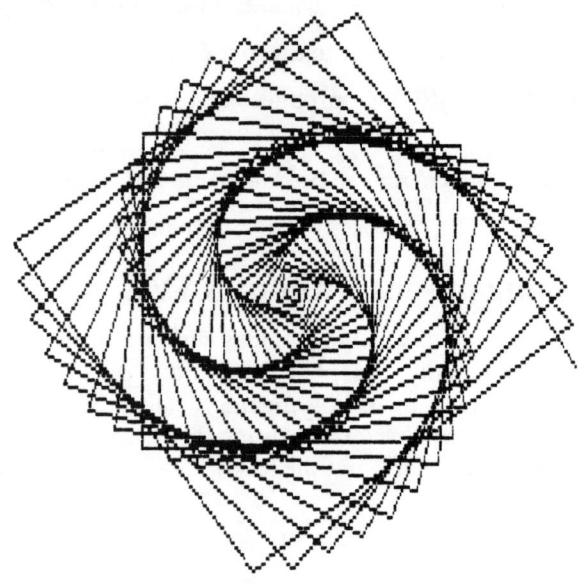

6 Recursion

6.1 What recursion does

Recursion is a wonderful and powerful feature of LOGO; not all computer languages can do recursion. It is enormously labour-saving – except for the Turtle!

You know that procedures can call other procedures; HOUSE calls SQUARE and TRIANGLE. A procedure can even call itself (or seem to). This is called *recursion*.

Make a simple procedure such as:

```
TO  LINE
FORWARD  200
BACK  200
END
```

Then incorporate this into a *recursive procedure*:

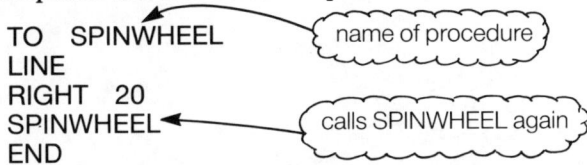

```
TO  SPINWHEEL
LINE
RIGHT  20
SPINWHEEL
END
```

Don't panic – you can stop the procedure executing by pressing ESCAPE.

6.2 What recursion really does

SPINWHEEL does not really call itself; it makes and calls *another copy* of itself. You can see on the next page what would happen if you could do SPINWHEEL one step at a time.

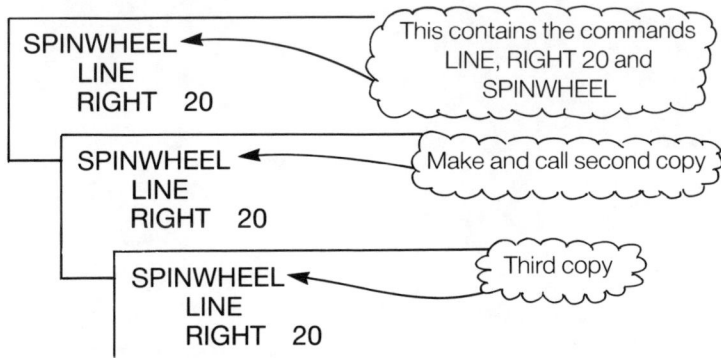

In theory, this process will never end; SPINWHEEL can always make and call another copy of itself. In practice, the computer may run out of memory eventually.

6.3 Projects

1. Try replacing the LINE of SPINWHEEL by something more exotic. You may need to change the angle as well.

2. The LINE procedure finished with the Turtle at the same place that it started. Try different effects of SPINWHEEL with procedures that do this and with those that do not.

3. Draw a SCRIBBLE something like this:
   Try this very simple recursion:

   ```
   TO   WHEEL
   SCRIBBLE
   WHEEL
   END
   ```

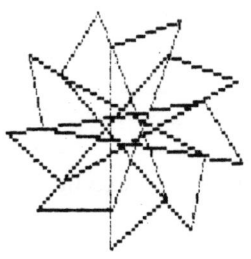

7 Polygons, stars and circles

7.1 Using recursion

Recursion is very powerful for drawing polygons, stars and circles. Try this:

```
TO   SQUARE
FORWARD   200
RIGHT   90
SQUARE
END
```

7.2 Project

Draw some other polygons and stars using recursion.

7.3 Heading

The Turtle's heading is the direction in which it is pointing. You can set the heading by using

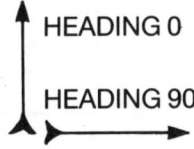

SETH   direction   (stands for SETHeading direction)

You can sometimes stop a recursion by *testing* the heading.

```
TO   ONESQUARE
FORWARD   200
RIGHT   90
IF   HEADING   =   0   [STOP]
ONESQUARE
END
```

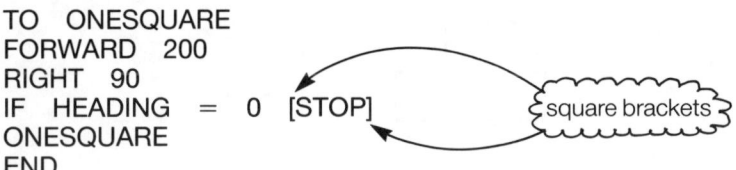

square brackets

7.4 Project

Does this method of stopping recursion work for stars?
Have you discovered the Turtle Total Trip Theorem for closed paths yet?

7.5 The Turtle Total Trip Theorem

An alternative method, which ensures that the procedure stops, is to replace the recursion by a procedure which uses REPEAT. To work out the number of REPEATs, you will find the Turtle Total Trip Theorem very useful.

The Turtle Total Trip Theorem just says that the total angle through which the Turtle turns in going round a closed path (back to the same position and heading) is a multiple of 360. When you draw a polygon or star using recursion, you can probably see how many times the Turtle has turned right round, and that will enable you to work out the number of REPEATs to create the same effect without recursion.

7.6 Circles

The Turtle only draws straight lines, but if you draw a polygon with enough sides, it looks very like a circle.

7.7 Projects

1. Experiment with circles.
   Draw a circle; draw a circle half the size, a quarter of the size . . .

2. Draw a truck.

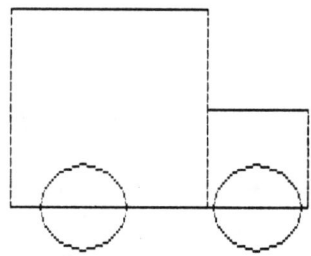

Draw a small truck – half size?

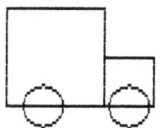

7.8 Drawing a circle with given radius (more advanced; involves using π)

Suppose you want to draw a circle of radius 200 by making a 36-sided polygon. The turn will have to be 10°, so you will need

```
TO CIRCLE
FORWARD ?
RIGHT 10
CIRCLE
END
```

The problem is how far forward to go. The complete circle (whose circumference is $2\pi \times$ radius) is to be drawn in 36 steps, so each step must be

$$\frac{2\pi \times 200}{36} = \frac{\pi \times 200}{18}$$

So you do:

```
TO   CIRCLE
FORWARD  200  *  3.14159  /  18
RIGHT  10
CIRCLE
END
```

The centre of this circle is very slightly above where the Turtle starts. If you want to line circles up alongside one another, a more accurate effect is produced by

```
TO   CIRCLE
RIGHT  5
FORWARD  200  *  3.14159  /  18
RIGHT  5
CIRCLE
END
```

To see why this is better, draw a hexagon as a *very* approximate circle by each of the following procedures:

```
TO   HEXAGON           TO   HEXAGON
FORWARD  200           RIGHT  30
RIGHT  60              FORWARD  200
HEXAGON                RIGHT  30
END                    HEXAGON
                       END
```

To ensure that the recursive procedure for a circle stops, insert a line to test the heading:

```
TO   CIRCLE
RIGHT  5
FORWARD  200  *  3.14159  /  18
RIGHT  5
IF   HEADING  =  0  [STOP]
CIRCLE
END
```

Alternatively, use REPEAT instead of recursion:

```
TO   CIRCLE
REPEAT  36  [RIGHT  5  FORWARD  200  *
   3.14159  /  18  RIGHT  5]
END
```

7.9 Projects

1. Make a procedure to draw a circle of given radius when the Turtle is sitting at the centre of it.
2. You will find the procedures RARC and LARC, which do quarter circles, very useful. Some dialects of LOGO provide these as primitives, but Logotron LOGO does not. Make your own procedures for RARC and LARC and do some combinations of them.

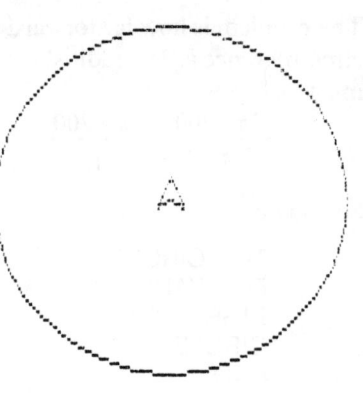

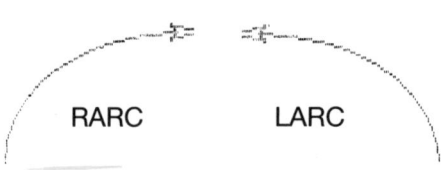

8 Variables

8.1 Varying the size of a drawing

At present, if you want to draw a square of a different size, you have to change the procedure. If you use *variables*, you can *input* the size of drawing you would like without changing the procedure.

Change the original version of SQUARE to use a variable. Start with

```
TO   SQUARE
REPEAT  4  [FORWARD  200  RIGHT  90]
END
```

Edit it to

```
TO  SQUAREINP   :SIDE
REPEAT  4  [FORWARD  :SIDE  RIGHT  90]
END
```

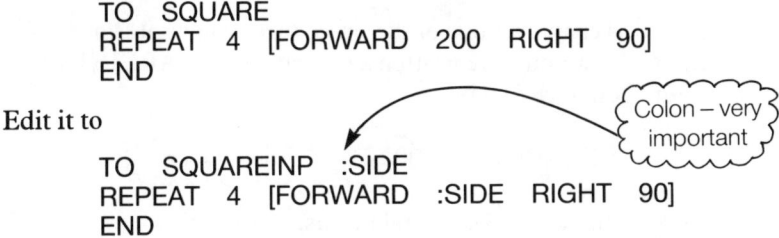

Colon – very important

Do not omit the colons; they are explained later in the chapter. When the procedure has been defined, it will say

```
SQUAREINP   defined
```

without the :SIDE, but if you try to run it, it will complain that it *does not have enough inputs*. Type

```
SQUAREINP   200
```

and it will run. You can use any number as the input.

8.2 Project

Make a procedure GROWSQUARE to draw this.

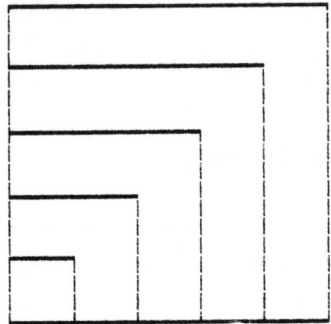

8.3 Procedures that take inputs

You will recall from Chapter 2 that some of the LOGO primitives take inputs. They include

> FORWARD
> BACK
> RIGHT
> LEFT

You have to type FORWARD 200 and so on. Other LOGO primitives do not take inputs; examples are:

> CS
> EDALL

Until this chapter, none of the procedures you wrote yourself took inputs. Now you have written a procedure SQUAREINP that takes an input. You have to type

> SQUAREINP 100

A procedure may take several inputs. Try this:

> TO RECTANGLE :HEIGHT :WIDTH
> REPEAT 2 [FD :HEIGHT RT 90 FD :WIDTH RT 90]
> END

To run this procedure, you have to give two inputs, so you type something like

> RECTANGLE   200   150

8.4 Project

Make procedures to draw:

> a house of given size
> a truck of given size

8.5 Colons and quotes

When you write

> TO   RECTANGLE   :HEIGHT   :WIDTH

LOGO does two things:

1. It sets up a procedure called RECTANGLE.

2. It associates with RECTANGLE two empty boxes called *variables*. LOGO gives those boxes the *names* "HEIGHT and "WIDTH.

```
┌─────────────────────────────────────────┐
│                  "HEIGHT      "WIDTH    │
│   RECTANGLE       ☐            ☐        │
└─────────────────────────────────────────┘
```

In LOGO, names (or *words*) always have a quotation mark " in front of them. You have used this earlier. To save your workspace, you typed something like

    SAVE   "SALLY

"SALLY is the *name* that you gave your workspace when you saved it. In the same way, the *names* of the variables in RECTANGLE are "HEIGHT and "WIDTH.

But *why are there colons* rather than quotes in the title of the procedure? The answer is that *a colon indicates the value* which is given to a variable, that is, the number which is put in the box. When you type RECTANGLE   200   150, the situation becomes:

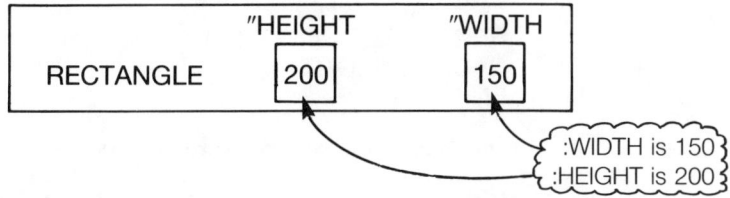

and the values in the boxes are 200 and 150. Thus, we give the procedure the title

    RECTANGLE   :HEIGHT   :WIDTH

to tell LOGO that RECTANGLE will use the *values* found in the boxes. Then

    RECTANGLE   200   150

tells LOGO that

    :HEIGHT is 200

and   :WIDTH is 150.

Within the procedure, the command FORWARD :HEIGHT instructs the procedure to look in the box named "HEIGHT, and to find and use the *value* of the variable – that is, 200. The punctuation gives LOGO important signals; "HEIGHT, :HEIGHT and HEIGHT mean three different things in LOGO.

    "HEIGHT   (pronounced quotes-height) is the *name* of a variable

:HEIGHT	(pronounced colon-height) is the *value* of the variable whose name is "HEIGHT
HEIGHT	without quotes or a colon is nothing to do with variables. LOGO always thinks that a word without a colon or quotes is a *procedure*

If you write HEIGHT without a colon in

    RECTANGLE :HEIGHT :WIDTH

LOGO will complain. It has looked for a procedure HEIGHT, and failed to find one.

8.6 Local variables

The boxes provided for variables in LOGO are *private*; their use is restricted to a particular procedure. They are called *local variables*, and they belong to that procedure only. Because the variables in LOGO are local, different procedures can use variables with the same name. Try this:

```
TO   FLAG   :HEIGHT
FORWARD   :HEIGHT
RECTANGLE   (:HEIGHT/2)   :HEIGHT
BACK   :HEIGHT
END
```

This is what happens when you do FLAG 200:

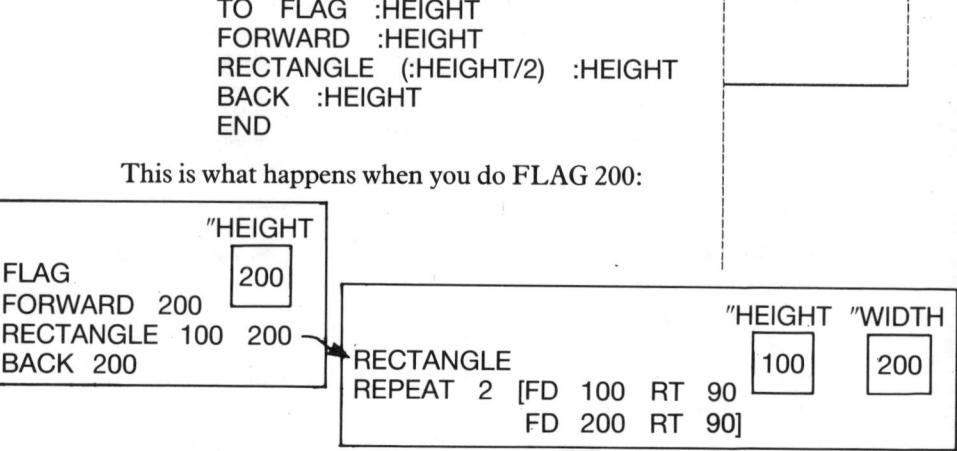

8.7 Coordinates

Instructions for moving the Turtle to a particular position on the screen are often useful. The screen has the coordinate system shown below.

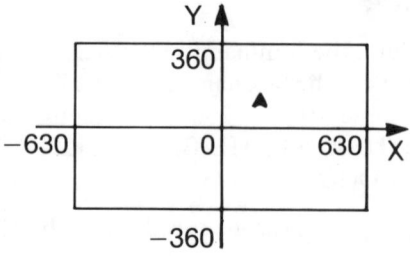

The commands

        SETX   number

and

        SETY   number

move the Turtle to given coordinates. For example,

        SETX   200
        SETY   100

will get the Turtle into the position shown in the diagram. Note that if the pen is down the Turtle draws a line as it moves.

You can move to new X- and Y-coordinates at the same time by using

        SETPOS

This command needs square brackets to enclose the *list* of the two coordinates to which the Turtle is to move, so

        SETPOS   [200   100]

produces the same effect as the last two commands, except that if the pen is down a line is drawn directly to the point. If you want to use variables with SETPOS, different syntax is needed. To move the Turtle to the point whose coordinates are stored in the variables named "ALONG and "UP, for example, you have to write

        SETPOS   SE   :ALONG   :UP

The reason for this is that LOGO does not allow you to write variables inside lists, so it objects to [:ALONG :UP]. However, the command

        SE   (stands for SEntence)

overcomes this problem by turning its inputs into a list. Thus

        SE   :ALONG   :UP

outputs a list whose members are the values of :ALONG and :UP, so that if for example

        :ALONG is 200

and   :UP is 150

then   SETPOS   SE   :ALONG   :UP

        is equivalent to SETPOS   [200   150].

8.8 Heading

The Turtle's *heading* is the direction in which it is pointing. You can set the heading using

    SETH   direction   (stands for SETHeading)

The heading is measured *clockwise* from the position where the Turtle starts from (i.e. facing upwards).

8.9 Projects

You are now ready to draw streets

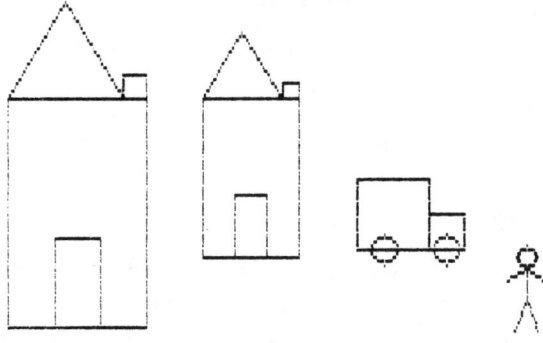

and all sorts of pictures.

9 MAKE and arithmetic

9.1 MAKE

In Chapter 8 you wrote a procedure GROWSQUARE to draw this. Probably you used a combination of two procedures which were something like these:

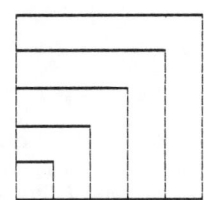

```
TO  SQUARE  :SIDE
REPEAT  4  [FORWARD  :SIDE  RIGHT  90]
END

TO  GROWSQUARE
SQUARE  20
SQUARE  40
SQUARE  60
SQUARE  80
SQUARE  100
END
```

This seems a rather tedious way of writing the solution to this problem. You might ask whether there is a way of changing the value of the variable named "SIDE automatically within GROWSQUARE, so that you can avoid typing SQUARE five times.

The LOGO primitive procedure

    MAKE

enables you to do this – it is used to put a value in a box such as "SIDE. Type:

    MAKE "SIDE 40
    PRINT :SIDE

The command

    MAKE "SIDE 40

tells LOGO to create a box whose name is "SIDE and put the number 40 in it.

    "SIDE
    [40]

When you ask the computer to PRINT :SIDE, it will print 40. The command

    PRINT   (abbr. PR)

prints out whatever you ask it to.

If a box whose name is "SIDE already exists, MAKE "SIDE puts a new value in the box. LOGO will even work out the value to put in that box. Try:

    MAKE   "SIDE (:SIDE + 50)
    PRINT   :SIDE

Did LOGO print out 90? It added 50 to the previous value in the "SIDE box, which should have been 40.

9.2 Project

Build a revised procedure for GROWSQUARE, using MAKE. A possible procedure is given below.

    TO   GROWSQUARE
    MAKE "SIDE 40
    REPEAT 5 [SQUARE :SIDE MAKE "SIDE (:SIDE
       + 40)]
    END

9.3 Arithmetic

In BBC LOGO, the notation for addition, subtraction, multiplication and division is straightforward. The arithmetical symbols are:

    + add
    − subtract
    * multiply
    / divide

However, the equals sign is not used in calculations. Instead of writing 3 + 4 =, you write

    PRINT   3 + 4

and LOGO responds by printing 7.

The command + does the calculation, but it does not print the result; + expects that some other procedure will be waiting to use the result of that calculation. For example, by using the command

    FORWARD (60 + 40)

you can see that the addition has been done. Try

    FORWARD (60 + 40)
    BACK   (110 - 10)

(The brackets are optional, but often aid legibility.) The Turtle should now be back where it started.

9.4 PRINT

The command

    PRINT   (abbr. PR)

enables you to see the result of a calculation without using the Turtle. PRINT takes *one input*, so it needs to be followed by that input, which is the *output* of an arithmetical operation, in this case. The diagram shows how PRINT 3 + 5 works.

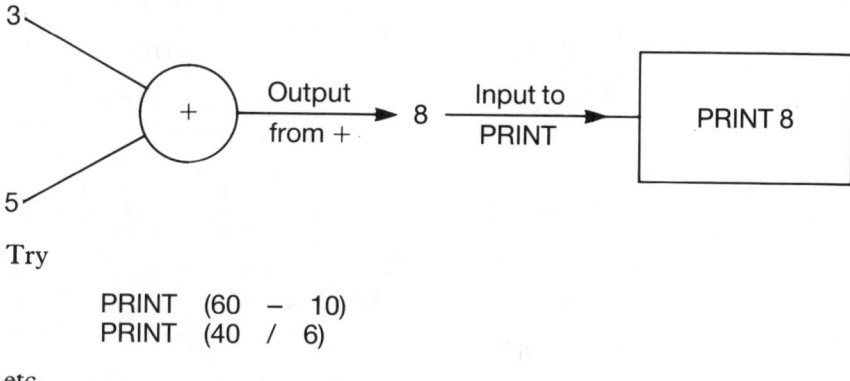

Try

    PRINT (60 - 10)
    PRINT (40 / 6)

etc.

9.5 Variables in arithmetical procedures

In a Turtle drawing procedure we can use variables to control the size of the drawing. For example, the procedure:

    TO HEXAGON :SIDE
    REPEAT 6 [FORWARD :SIDE RIGHT 60]
    END

draws a hexagon of side 60 when you type HEXAGON 60.

In just the same way, we can use variables in arithmetical procedures. For example, we can build the procedure below, called ADDTHREE, to add three numbers; this procedure will take three inputs.

    TO ADDTHREE :A :B :C
    OP :A + :B + :C
    END

We have used the primitive OP in this program. The primitive

    OP   (stands for OutPut)

takes one input and it does three things:

(i)   it stops the procedure in which it is used, and returns control to the procedure which called it;

(ii) at the same time it takes its input, which may itself be a complicated procedure, and works it out;

(iii) it passes the *output* of that working out to the procedure which called it.

For example,

    PRINT ADDTHREE 5 7 9

does the things shown in the diagram:

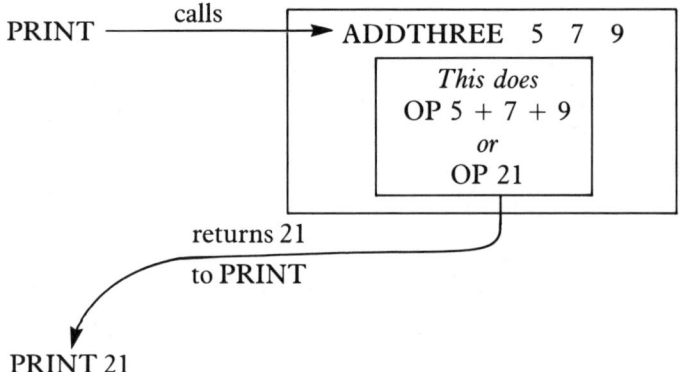

The procedure ADDTHREE is rather trivial, but in more complicated cases there are advantages in using sub-procedures which send back an OP to the main procedure. For example, the same procedure ADDTHREE can be used in all the following examples without change

    PRINT ADDTHREE 5 7 9
    FORWARD ADDTHREE 5 7 9
    REPEAT (ADDTHREE 5 7 9) [SQUARE RIGHT 40]

9.6 Projects

In these projects, you will probably want to use TEXTSCREEN, as they do not involve any drawing.

1. Make a procedure to find the perimeter of a rectangle (that is, the distance all the way round it). When you type

    PRINT   RECT.PERIM   6   5

   it should respond 22.

2. Make a procedure to find the area of a rectangle (that is, the number of unit squares that would cover it). When you type

    PRINT   RECT.AREA   6   5

   it should respond 30.

3. Make procedures to find the area and perimeter of a square. Use RECT.AREA and RECT.PERIM as subroutines. When you type

    PRINT   SQ.AREA   6

   and   PRINT   SQ.PERIM   6

   it should respond 36 and 24 respectively.

4. Print out a list of the squares of numbers from 1 to 20.

10 More commands using numbers

10.1 RANDOM

There is a useful facility in LOGO for playing games and for drawing unexpected designs.

    RANDOM

takes one input and returns a random whole number. For example,

    PRINT   RANDOM 6

prints a random whole number chosen from 0, 1, 2, 3, 4, 5. Hence, the commands

    PRINT   (RANDOM 6) + 1

can be used to simulate throwing a die. The brackets are necessary here. If you leave them out, and write

    PRINT   RANDOM 6 + 1

LOGO will work out 6 + 1 first, and think that you mean to do

    PRINT   RANDOM 7

10.2 Other arithmetical commands

It is sometimes useful to be able to get rid of the decimal part of a number such as 6.66667. This can be done in two ways; the command

    PRINT   INT   6.66667

chops off the decimal part, and prints 6. Alternatively, ROUND rounds the number to the nearest whole number, so

    PRINT   ROUND   6.6667

prints 7 as its result.

LOGO can evaluate square roots; the command is

    SQRT   number

Thus, PRINT   SQRT   225

prints out 15.

LOGO can also do trigonometry. If you need this facility, consult the *Logotron LOGO Manual* for details.

10.3 Integer division

If you type

    PRINT   9   /   4

then LOGO will respond with 2.25, which may surprise a child who thinks that

    9/4 = 2 remainder 1.

There are commands which produce these results; the command

    QUOT   9   4

produces the whole number quotient 2. You can get the remainder by using

    REMAINDER   9   4

which produces 1.

10.4 Prefix arithmetic

There are additional arithmetical commands in BBC LOGO, which are of a different type from the ordinary arithmetical commands – they are *prefix commands*. The commands QUOT and REMAINDER are of this type. The other prefix arithmetic commands do the same jobs as the ordinary arithmetical commands, but their syntax is different. To add 25 and 12, you can use

    SUM   25   12

instead of 25 + 12. The command SUM is written first, followed by its two inputs; thus the command is *prefix*ed to the inputs. There are three prefix arithmetic commands which can be used instead of the ordinary arithmetical commands if you wish. They are

    SUM
    PROD
    DIV

The reason that these commands are provided in BBC LOGO is to enable the language to be used consistently, because all the non-arithmetical LOGO commands are prefix. You write

    FORWARD   50

putting the command before the inputs.

The ordinary arithmetical commands, such as +, are *infix*; you put the command *in between* its inputs, as in

    PRINT   3   +   4

Thus, the arithmetical commands are an exception to the general rule that in LOGO, commands are prefixed to their inputs.

10.5 Projects

1. Write a procedure AVERAGE which takes two inputs, so that

       PRINT   AVERAGE   12   20

   prints 16.

2. Draw a rectangle whose height is half its width. Use this to draw a flag of given size, such as

       FLAG   50

   Spin the flag.

3. Draw a square at a random position on the screen. (You can use a combination of SETPOS and RANDOM, for example.)
   Make the square of random size. Also alter the pen colour with SETPC   RANDOM   6. Use a recursive procedure to draw a lot of random squares.

4. (Harder) Draw a square of given size and its diagonals. If you know Pythagoras' Theorem, this will help you to work out the lengths of the diagonals; otherwise, trial and error methods will be needed.

5. Simulate a die. When you type TOSS, it will draw a picture of the face, showing a random number of spots. Design each face first. You will need a *test* to decide which face is to be displayed; see the next section.

10.6 IF – and tests

Often, you want LOGO to do different actions according to whether some condition is satisfied or not. For example, when drawing random squares on the screen, you may not want to draw a square which will be partly wrapped round to the other side of the screen. The command needed to make a choice between actions is

    IF –

The syntax of this command is

    IF   *test*   [*actions*]   [*actions*]

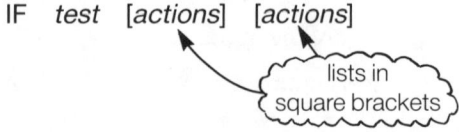

lists in square brackets

For example, you might use the line

    IF   HEADING   =   0   [RIGHT   90   STOP]   [LEFT   90]

The lists of actions must be enclosed in square brackets.

A *test* is a question which returns the answer TRUE or FALSE. If the *test* returns the answer TRUE then the first list of actions is carried out. If the test returns FALSE then the second list of actions is carried out.

The second list of actions may be omitted, so that the command reads:

    IF   [*test*]   [*actions*]

In this case, if the test returns FALSE, the program goes straight on to the next line.

To make IF work, we need tests which return TRUE/FALSE answers. A comparison between two numbers using <,> or = gives a way of doing this. For example,

    5>2 is TRUE

and   3+2=5 is TRUE,

but   5>7 is FALSE.

LOGO is able to make comparisons such as this, so that we can use commands such as

    IF   :X   <   90   [SETX   :X]

    IF   :X   >   90   [SETX   (120   −   :X)]

and   IF   :X   =   3   [THREES]

11 Words and lists

11.1 A larger project

For very young children, the full computer keyboard, and the amount of typing involved in using the full version of LOGO, may be too difficult. However, they can still enjoy using LOGO, particularly if a Floor Turtle is available to them.

What is needed is a simplified version of LOGO, which uses a single key to represent each of FORWARD, BACK, RIGHT and LEFT. The space bar should not be needed, and pressing a single number key should produce a larger movement of the Turtle than in the full LOGO, so that children will really notice that the Turtle has moved. Then brightly coloured labels can be stuck over the few keys that are to be used, to help the children to find them. You may not even want children to need to use the RETURN key, although we find it useful. We have re-labelled the RETURN key of the computer as GO, and children soon learn that only when they press GO will anything happen.

You will have your own ideas about exactly what features you would want to build in to your own version of YOUNGLOGO. One of the exciting features of LOGO is that not only does it do Turtle graphics; it is a high-level computing language which enables you to write software such as YOUNGLOGO to your own design.

The next few chapters show you how to use features of LOGO which are not needed for Turtle graphics; however, you do need them for writing software such as YOUNGLOGO and educational games. We shall introduce these additional LOGO commands as we start you off on designing and writing your own version of YOUNGLOGO.

11.2 Input from the keyboard

In YOUNGLOGO, you will want a child to input a single letter such as F from the keyboard to the program, and LOGO will need to translate that to FORWARD and use it to drive the Turtle. The command which enables LOGO to accept input from the keyboard is:

    RL   (stands for ReadList)

To see how RL works, build this little experimental procedure:

```
TO  TRY
    PRINT  [TYPE  SOMETHING]
    MAKE   "TXT  RL
    PRINT  :TXT
    TRY
END
```
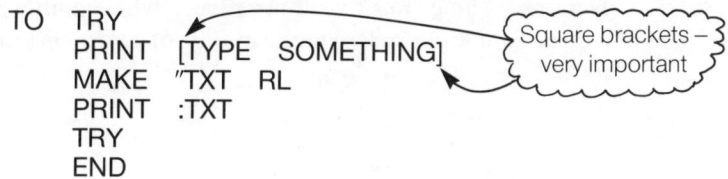

When you run TRY, the words TYPE SOMETHING are printed on the screen, and the procedure then waits for you to type something in at the keyboard and press RETURN. Whatever you type goes into the "TXT box. The procedure TRY is a recursive procedure, so it will keep asking you to type something in until you use ESCAPE.

Try different sorts of input when TRY asks you to type something. Include:

> words,
> phrases,
> numbers,
> nothing at all.

The command RL works like this:

1. RL stops and waits for you to input some characters at the keyboard.

2. RL *outputs* your typing, stored in a list (see para. 11.3). So if you type HELLO, the command RL outputs the list [HELLO].

In TRY, the output of RL goes into the "TXT box, as if the line were

```
MAKE  "TXT  [HELLO]
```

11.3 Lists

Square brackets are an essential part of LOGO; they indicate that you are dealing with some data in the form of a *list*. A list always has square brackets surrounding it. Here are some examples of lists:

```
[TYPE  SOMETHING]
[HELLO]
[WHAT  DO  YOU  WANT?]
[243]
[2  4  3]
[46  RAMBLE  12.76]
[SUNDAY  MONDAY  TUESDAY  WEDNESDAY
   THURSDAY  FRIDAY  SATURDAY]
[]
```

The elements of a list can be *numbers*, *words* or other *lists*. The easiest of these three *data types* to recognise is a *number*.

A number can be positive or negative, a whole number or a decimal. You must not put spaces in the middle of a number; these are valid numbers:

    254
    −254
    254.123
    −254.123

11.4 Words

A *word* is any sequence of characters which starts with a *quotation mark*. LOGO recognises the beginning of a word by the quotation mark, and it recognises that it has come to the end of a word when it comes to a space. This means that you can mix up letters, figures and punctuation marks in a word. These are valid words:

    "HELLO
    "LINE2
    "WANT?
    "2+3
    "GOODB?YE
    "...
    ",,,

This explains why you so often have to use the quotation mark in LOGO. The *name of a variable* is a word, so you type:

    MAKE "HEIGHT 50

When you name your workspace and save it with

    SAVE "SALLY

then "SALLY is a word.

However, when you command LOGO to execute a primitive procedure, by typing

    PENUP or FORWARD 50

or when you run a procedure you have built yourself, such as SQUARE 200, you do not use a quotation mark. Commands which are executed do not have a quote; it is only words which have quotes at the beginning.

You can type a word in directly at the keyboard, as in

    PRINT "HELLO

However, if you type HELLO without a quote, LOGO thinks it is a *procedure* rather than a word, and so it complains:

    I DON'T KNOW HOW TO HELLO

Thus, the quote distinguishes between a word and a procedure which is to be executed. The idea of using a quote to do this is borrowed from LISP, from which LOGO is descended. In LISP, every expression is treated as a procedure, and LISP tries to carry it out, or *evaluate* it, unless it is preceded by a quote. Thus, in LISP,

> a quote inhibits evaluation.

This is also a helpful way of thinking about quotes in LOGO.

> **A quote stops LOGO from trying to find and carry out a procedure with that name.**

Thus, the quote in "HELLO is not part of the word, but a signal to LOGO that "HELLO is a word, not a procedure to be executed.

In LOGO, square brackets also inhibit evaluation. If you type:

```
PRINT  [SAY   HELLO]
```

LOGO prints the list [SAY   HELLO], but *without the brackets*, and does not try to look for procedures called SAY and HELLO.

It is important to keep in mind the fact that PRINT prints a list without its outer square brackets, and a word without the " at the beginning. The primitive

```
SHOW
```

does exactly the same as PRINT, except that it prints square brackets when they exist. Try these:

```
PRINT  [SAY   HELLO]
SHOW   [SAY   HELLO]
PRINT  "HELLO
SHOW   "HELLO
```

11.5 Project

The error messages in LOGO vary according to the type of error, as you know. This can help you to distinguish between words and lists. Observe the effect of various commands such as:

```
PRINT   "HELLO
SHOW    HELLO
PRINT   [HELLO]
SHOW    :HELLO
PRINT   [ ]
```

11.6 Variables and their values

The name of a variable is a word, such as "TXT. The command

MAKE "TXT expression ⟵ {number, word or list}

creates a box labelled "TXT, and puts the *expression* into that box as the *value of the variable*. LOGO is extremely kind, compared with other computer languages, about the expressions which it will accept as values of variables. Experiment in putting different types of expression into the "TXT box.

Did you find that LOGO will accept a *number*, or a *word*, or a *list*, and put it in the "TXT box? The ability of LOGO to accept any data-type and put it into a variable box is very useful. From now onwards, we shall use *expression* to stand for any of a *number*, a *word* or a *list*.

LOGO can also test to see which data-type is in a variable box. Try this procedure:

```
TEST :TYPE
    IF LIST? :TYPE [PRINT [LIST]]
    IF WORD? :TYPE [PRINT [WORD]]
    IF NUMBER? :TYPE [PRINT [NUMBER]]
END
```

Use different values for the variable "TYPE, so that you try examples such as

```
TEST 20
TEST [HELLO THERE]
TEST [HELLO]
```

and others.

Three new LOGO primitives were used in this procedure. They are

LIST?, WORD? and NUMBER?

Each *tests* to see if its input is of its own type. The syntax is

LIST? expression

LIST? returns TRUE if the expression is a list, and FALSE otherwise. Hence, LIST? is a *test* which provides the TRUE or FALSE output which IF – needs as its input. The syntax of WORD? and NUMBER? is similar. Notice that a number is regarded as both a word and a number.

11.7 Projects

1. Start to build the procedures which will make up YOUNGLOGO. TRY is the basis of YOUNGLOGO. Design a nice prompt which sits on the screen when YOUNGLOGO is waiting for you to type something in. Arrange (temporarily) for YOUNGLOGO to print

FORWARD when you type in F, BACK when you type in B, and to ignore any other input. To do this, you need to know that the equals sign = is a test which not only tests *numbers* for equality; it can also be used to test *words* or *lists* to see if they are the same.

2. Amend YOUNGLOGO so that it will stop gracefully without using ESCAPE. It should stop if you type in some special word such as EXIT. Thus, EXIT will apparently become a primitive command in YOUNGLOGO; the function of EXIT is to return you to LOGO.

11.8 Laying out text on the screen

Another type of project which is possible now that you can use RL is to write an interactive arithmetical program. For example, a program may ask a child to input a number at the keyboard, and the procedure will then print out the multiplication table for that number.

The screen layout may be a bit tiresome, but the following points should help.

You can clear the textscreen by using

    CT   (stands for ClearText)

and start the printing at a particular place on the textscreen by using

    SETCURSOR

SETCURSOR takes a list with two elements as input; the first element is the column and the second the line number, as shown in the diagram below.

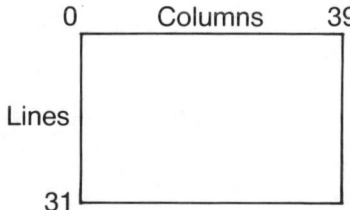

The command

    SETCURSOR [20 15]

puts the cursor in the centre of the screen.

The command

    TYPE

is just like PRINT, except that the cursor does not move to the next line after printing.

The commands PRINT and TYPE normally take only one input. However, they can be persuaded to take as many inputs as you like by enclosing the whole printing command in brackets, like this:

(PRINT "HOW "ARE "YOU)

The command PRINT " produces a blank line.

11.9 Projects

1. Print out some multiplication tables. (You may need to read the next chapter to cope with some of the problems you will encounter.)

2. Write an interactive arithmetic program.

12 Tearing lists apart

12.1 Further development of YOUNGLOGO

When YOUNGLOGO is running, a child's input from the keyboard will be something like:

    F7

You will want the Turtle to respond by doing something like:

    FORWARD 350

In this chapter we look at the commands which enable you to make YOUNGLOGO do this.

12.2 Tearing lists apart

In Project 2 of para. 11.7, you have probably arranged to store the child's input from the keyboard in a box called "TXT.

    "TXT
    | [F7] |

A likely method of proceeding with the YOUNGLOGO project is to get LOGO to do something like this: look at the first character of the list in "TXT to see if it is F, and the second character to verify that it is a numerical character. Then you will need to get LOGO to build up the command

    FORWARD 350

and tell the Turtle to carry out this command.

    LOGO provides commands which take lists apart. Our list has only *one element*, the word "F7. However, a young child might manage to get a list with many elements into the "TXT box; for instance if lots of keys (including the space bar) were randomly pressed, he or she would end up with something like this:

    "TXT
    | [RS   23   46A   P   BX;] |

This list has five elements. A child may also manage to get the *empty list* [] into "TXT, if he or she hits ENTER before doing anything else. The empty list has no elements.

The commands FIRST and BF (stands for ButFirst) are used to split off bits of lists and look at them. Try:

```
PRINT  FIRST  [HELLO HOW ARE YOU?]
PRINT  BUTFIRST  [HELLO HOW ARE YOU?]
```

Also try commands such as the following, until you know how FIRST and BF work with lists, words and numbers:

```
PRINT  FIRST  "HELLO
PRINT  FIRST  123.4
PRINT  BF  "HELLO
PRINT  BF  123.4
PRINT  FIRST  [ ]
```

12.3 FIRST and BF

The behaviour of the command:

FIRST expression ⟵ *number, word or list*

can be described as follows:

(i) If *expression* is a *list*, FIRST returns the *word* which is the first element of the list. FIRST gives an error message if the list is empty.

(ii) If *expression* is a *word* or a *number*, FIRST returns the *character* which is the first character of the word. FIRST gives an error message if the word is empty. We recall that in many ways, LOGO treats numbers as if they were words. Notice what happens, however, if you do

```
PRINT  FIRST  0.123
```

The behaviour of the command

```
BF  expression
```

is rather similar to that of FIRST, except that the result of deleting the first element of a list is a list, and the result of deleting the first element of a word is a word:

(i) If *expression* is a *list*, BF returns a *list* consisting of all the elements except the first element of the list. It gives an error message if the original list is empty.

(ii) If *expression* is a *word* or a *number*, BF returns a *word* containing all the characters except the first character of the word. It gives an error message if the original word is empty.

You can print the *character* which is the first character of the first word of a non-empty list stored in "TXT by doing:

```
PRINT  FIRST  FIRST  :TXT
```

For example, if "TXT contains the list [F7], then FIRST :TXT produces the word F7, and so FIRST (FIRST :TXT) produces the character F. Similarly, the second character of the list in "TXT can be produced by doing:

```
PRINT  FIRST  BF  FIRST  :TXT
```

Here, BF (FIRST :TXT) produces the list [7], and so

```
FIRST  BF  FIRST  :TXT
```

produces the character 7.

12.4 Project

As the next step towards YOUNGLOGO, build a procedure BABYLOGO, which might be a child's first introduction to LOGO. It should do these things:

(i) ignore an empty input from the keyboard;

(ii) move the Turtle FORWARD 50 if the first letter of the keyboard input is F, and move the Turtle BACK 50 if the first letter of the keyboard input is B;

(iii) turn the Turtle RIGHT 45 if the first letter of the keyboard input is R, and turn the Turtle LEFT 45 if the first letter of the keyboard input is L;

(iv) return to LOGO if the keyboard input is EXIT;

(v) ignore any other keyboard input.

12.5 Other commands which manipulate lists

The following commands may also be useful:

```
LAST and BL        (stands for ButLast)
```

behave similarly to FIRST and BF, at the other end of a list.

The command

```
LIST
```

takes any number of inputs and outputs them as a list. For example

```
SHOW  LIST  "HELLO  "THERE
```

creates and prints the list

```
[HELLO  THERE]
```

The command

    SE   (stands for SEntence)

works nearly the same as LIST, except that any constituent lists are broken down into pieces first. The commands

    MAKE "X SE "A [1 2 3]

puts the list

    [A 1 2 3]

in "X.

12.6 Commands which take brackets

SE is one of several commands which normally take *two* inputs, but you can fool them into taking more than two inputs by using brackets. If, in the last section, you had written

    MAKE "X SE "A [1 2 3] "B

LOGO would have complained about "B. The first input to SE is "A, and the second is [1 2 3]. SE does not expect a third input.

However, if you enclose *the command and its inputs* in round brackets, LOGO will no longer complain; many of its commands can be persuaded to take more than the usual number of inputs by the use of round brackets.

In this manual we have used the following primitives which can be persuaded to take more than the usual number of inputs by surrounding them and their inputs with round brackets:

    SE
    LIST
    TYPE
    SUM
    PROD

For example, SUM normally takes two inputs, but

    PRINT (SUM 2 3 4 5)

will work, although LOGO complains about the 4 in

    PRINT SUM 2 3 4 5

One command which cannot be persuaded to take more than two inputs by the use of brackets is LIST. If you need to use more than two inputs to LIST, you have to repeat the command, as in

    PRINT LIST (LIST "A "B) "C

13 Single key input

13.1 RC

BABYLOGO teaches a child that he can make the Turtle move by pressing one of the keys F, B, R or L and then hitting ENTER. The amount by which the Turtle moves is pre-determined in the procedure. The next step in a child's learning may be to get him to press F, B, R or L followed by a number key which controls how far the Turtle moves. It is quite easy to design a procedure to do this by splitting off the second character of the list in "TXT, looking at it to see that it is a number, and using it to control the Turtle's movement. This procedure indicates what is needed:

```
DISTANCE
MAKE   "TXT  RL
MAKE   "MOVE  FIRST  BF  FIRST  :TXT
IF  NOT  NUMBER?  :MOVE  [STOP]
FORWARD  (50  *  :MOVE)
END
```

This puts the second character of :TXT in the "MOVE box

The child still has to press ENTER, however, to make the Turtle move. The primitive

       RC   (stands for ReadCharacter)

enables you to get the Turtle to move *immediately* a single number key has been pressed.

RC waits for a *single* key to be pressed, and outputs a single-character word containing it. It accepts the input instantly, and does not wait for ENTER to be pressed. To see how RC works, build this procedure and try it out by pressing various keys:

```
INPUT
MAKE   "A   RC
PRINT  :A
PRINT  NUMBER?  :A
INPUT
END
```

The test given by NUMBER? enables the procedure to decide whether a word consisting of a letter or a number has been stored in "A. When RC encounters a non-printing key, such as ENTER or the space bar, the empty word is returned and so is stored in "A.

You are now ready to build YOUNGLOGO. You can store the first two characters that a child inputs in two different boxes, called "DIR and "MOVE, by using the commands:

    MAKE   "DIR   RC
    MAKE   "MOVE   RC

A keyboard input of F7 will now produce:

    "DIR   "MOVE
    | F | | 7 |

You can then look in "DIR to see which command the Turtle is to execute, and look in "MOVE for the number which is used to calculate how much the Turtle is to move.

13.2 ASCII codes

If you follow the approach suggested in the last paragraph, the child will no longer need to press ENTER; the Turtle will move as soon as two suitable keys have been pressed. However, you may still want to use ENTER for some purposes; for example, you may want to exit gracefully from YOUNGLOGO if a certain combination of keys is pressed, such as X (ENTER). If you want to do this, you have to arrange for YOUNGLOGO to recognise ENTER. ASCII codes give a way of achieving this.

All the symbols shown on the keyboard are related to code numbers known as ASCII codes (American Standard Code for Information Interchange), and LOGO provides the primitive

    ASCII

which returns the ASCII code of a character. Try this procedure:

```
CODE
MAKE   "A  RC
PRINT  ASCII  :A
IF  (ASCII  :A)  =  13  [STOP]
CODE
END
```

Press each key on the keyboard in turn, so as to get a list of ASCII codes. The following codes enable you to distinguish between an input of different non-printing keys:

    ENTER has code 13
    SPACE has code 32

A complete list of ASCII codes is given in the Appendix of the *BBC User Guide*.

13.3 Project

You are now able to complete YOUNGLOGO. When finished, it should be able to draw FORWARD and BACK, and to turn RIGHT and LEFT by appropriate multiples of the keyboard input. You may also want to add other features, such as PENUP and PENCOLOR. You will also want it to exit gracefully to LOGO when you type some special characters such as X (ENTER).

13.4 KEY?

The command KEY? tests whether a key is being pressed, and so it can be used to start or stop LOGO doing something. Try this procedure:

```
DRAW
IF  KEY?  [FORWARD  2]
DRAW
END
```

The Turtle crawls forward while you are pressing any key. KEY? is a *test*, and returns FALSE if no key is being pressed, and TRUE if a key is being pressed. KEY? does not look to see what key is being pressed; if you want LOGO to read the key, you have to use RC. Try this change in the DRAW procedure:

```
DRAW
IF  NOT  RC  =  "R  [FORWARD  2]
IF  RC  =  "R  [RIGHT  90]
DRAW
END
```

13.5 Project

Develop a piece of software which draws on the screen while keys are held down; ensure that you can steer the Turtle by pressing different keys.

14 Boolean primitives

14.1 The primitive NOT

In the procedure DISTANCE, which you tried in para. 13.1, the primitive NOT was used in the following way:

    IF   NOT   NUMBER?   :MOVE   [STOP]

The command NOT is an example of a *Boolean primitive*; these primitives are used to carry out 'logical operations'. We recall that the command

    IF –

requires either TRUE or FALSE as its input. The command NOT outputs either TRUE or FALSE; if the input to NOT is TRUE then the output is FALSE, and vice versa. To see how this works, try:

    PRINT   NOT   LIST?   [HELLO   THERE]

This will print FALSE, because [HELLO THERE] is a list, and so the output of LIST? [HELLO THERE] is TRUE.

Thus, in the procedure DISTANCE, NOT was used to do something if the box "MOVE did not contain a number. For example, suppose the box "MOVE contained K:

    "MOVE
    | K |

Then the test

    NUMBER?   :MOVE

would give FALSE as its output, and

    NOT   NUMBER?   :MOVE

would give TRUE. Hence,

    IF   NOT   NUMBER?   :MOVE   [STOP]

would then stop the procedure of which it was part, and return control to the procedure which called it.

14.2 AND and OR

There are three Boolean primitives in all; the others are AND and OR.

These commands require *two* inputs, which must be either TRUE or FALSE. Their behaviour is as follows:

The primitive AND returns TRUE if *both* its inputs are true, and FALSE otherwise.

The primitive OR returns TRUE if *either* (or *both*) of its inputs is true, and FALSE otherwise.

Both AND and OR are *prefix* commands; they must be written before their inputs. They enable you to test combinations of conditions at the same time. For example, the line:

　　　　IF　AND　(:A　>　0)　(:A　<　10)　[STOP]

stops the procedure if 0<A<10, while the line:

　　　　IF　OR　:A　>　10　:A　<　0　[STOP]

stops the procedure if A>10 or A<0.

AND and OR can be fooled into taking more than their normal two inputs by using brackets around the command and its inputs. For example, you can write

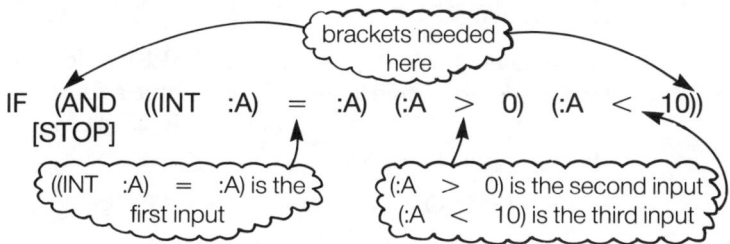

14.3 Commands which use TRUE or FALSE

We have used several commands which *output* either TRUE or FALSE. They are:

>	LIST?	AND
<	NUMBER?	OR
=	WORD?	NOT

Other similar commands are the following:

　　　　EMPTY?

tests a word or list to see if it is empty;

　　　　EQUAL?

is a prefix form of the equals sign;

　　　　MEMBER?

looks to see if its first input is a member of the list which is its second input.

There are also several commands which need TRUE or FALSE as *inputs*. These are the control command:

IF (TRUE or FALSE)

and the Boolean primitives:

NOT (TRUE or FALSE)
AND (TRUE or FALSE) (TRUE or FALSE)
OR   (TRUE or FALSE) (TRUE or FALSE)

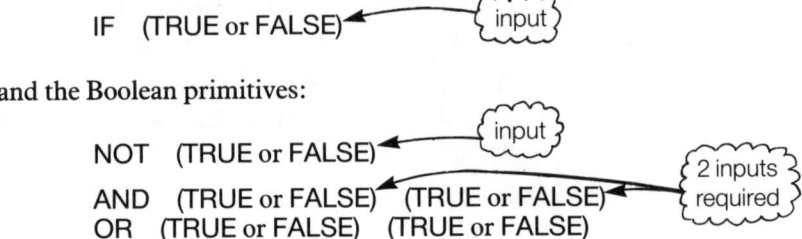

The Boolean primitives produce *outputs* which are also TRUE/FALSE.

14.4 Building your own tests

A command which requires TRUE/FALSE as its input does not care where that input comes from. It may come as the output of another command, or you can type it in yourself, as the *word* "TRUE or "FALSE. The two lines:

IF NOT 1 = 2 [BABYLOGO]

and   IF "TRUE [BABYLOGO]

have exactly the same effect; BABYLOGO is carried out. Because you can type in "TRUE or "FALSE, LOGO enables you to build your own test procedures; you can devise tests that were not provided as primitives. For example, the primitive NUMBER? tests whether a variable is a number; however, no primitive is provided to test whether a variable is a *whole* number. The procedure given below will do this.

INT? :X
IF (INT :X) = :X [OP "TRUE] [OP "FALSE]
END

As another example of a home-made test, try the following procedure to test whether a number is even:

EVEN? :N
IF (REMAINDER :N 2) = 0 [OP "TRUE] [OP "FALSE]
END

14.5 Projects

1. Make a procedure to check whether one number is divisible by another.

2. Make procedures to test whether a number is prime. Print out a list of prime numbers.

3. Make a procedure to work out the *absolute value* of a number. The absolute value of a negative number is the corresponding positive number; for example:

    abs (−3)=3
    abs (3)=3

15 More about variables

15.1 Polygons with recursion with variables

In Chapter 7 you drew some polygons and stars using recursion; for example:

```
TO   HEXAGON
     FORWARD   200
     RIGHT  60
     HEXAGON
     END
```

You can combine this with the use of a variable to draw a hexagon of any size:

```
TO   HEXAGON   :SIDE
     FORWARD   :SIDE   RIGHT   60
     HEXAGON   :SIDE
     END
```

Note that the second copy of HEXAGON needs an input

Here is an all-purpose polygon, star and circle drawing procedure.

```
TO   POLY   :SIDE   :ANGLE
     FORWARD   :SIDE
     RIGHT   :ANGLE
     POLY   :SIDE   :ANGLE
     END
```

15.2 Polyspirals

Polyspirals are like polygons, except that they grow.

```
TO   POLYSPI   :SIDE   :ANGLE
     FORWARD   :SIDE
     RIGHT   :ANGLE
     POLYSPI   (:SIDE   +   10)   :ANGLE
     END
```

15.3 Projects

1. What different shapes will POLY draw?
2. Try POLYSPI with different angle inputs. Some of the best designs are produced by angles near, but not equal to, the angles that make polygons and stars. For instance, try

```
POLYSPI  1  120
POLYSPI  1  118
POLYSPI  1  122
```

3. Try some variations on POLYSPI, such as the following:

```
TO  POLYSPI2  :SIDE  :ANGLE  :INC
    IF  :SIDE  =  500  [STOP]
    FORWARD  :SIDE
    RIGHT  :SIDE
    POLYSPI2  (:SIDE  +  :INC)  :ANGLE  :INC
    END
```

In this procedure, INC stands for *increase*, and an extra line has been put in to stop the procedure automatically.

Also use a DEC to make the POLYSPI spiral inwards.

4. INSPI is a variation which changes the angle, rather than the side (the names POLY, POLYSPI and INSPI are traditional in LOGO circles).

```
TO  INSPI  :SIDE  :ANGLE
    FORWARD  :SIDE
    RIGHT  :ANGLE
    INSPI  :SIDE  (:ANGLE  +  10)
    END
```

Try INSPI 50 33, INSPI 50 40 and others. Amend INSPI to use an INC, so that you have

```
INSPI  :SIDE  :ANGLE  :INC
```

Experiment.

15.4 Local variables

LOGO uses two types of variables: *local variables* and *global variables*. To prevent surprises in the behaviour of programs, you need to know how they differ. A *local variable* in LOGO is a box which belongs only to the procedure in which it occurs. Any other procedures in your workspace cannot find that box or look inside it. This fact is very important, because it means that different procedures can use the same names for variables which mean different things. To see how this works, try these procedures.

```
TO  TRYOUT  :SIDE
    FORWARD  :SIDE
    RIGHT  90
    ALTER  :SIDE
    FORWARD  :SIDE
    END
```

```
TO ALTER :SIDE
   MAKE "SIDE (:SIDE + 100)
   FORWARD :SIDE
   RIGHT 90
   END
```

Do TRYOUT 50. Were you surprised that the third line you drew was of length 50 rather than 150? In ALTER, :SIDE was increased from 50 to 150, but in TRYOUT, which drew the third line, :SIDE stayed at 50.

Here is how the variables work in the two procedures. When the name of a variable appears in the *title line* of a procedure, LOGO creates a box to hold the variable. The box only belongs to that particular procedure – no other procedure can find it or look in it. It is *local*. So in the title line TRYOUT :SIDE, a box labelled "SIDE is created for TRYOUT. Similarly, in the title line of ALTER :SIDE, a box labelled "SIDE is created for ALTER. These boxes have the same labels, but they are different boxes, and they can contain different values. When you type TRYOUT 50, LOGO puts 50 in the "SIDE box belonging to TRYOUT. When TRYOUT reaches the line ALTER :SIDE, it reads it as ALTER 50, and moves over to the procedure ALTER, putting 50 in the box labelled "SIDE in ALTER.

The line of ALTER

```
MAKE "SIDE (:SIDE + 100)
```

looks to see if there is a box in ALTER labelled "SIDE – there is, so it calculates the new value to put in that "SIDE box, and puts it there. The diagram shows how the whole thing works.

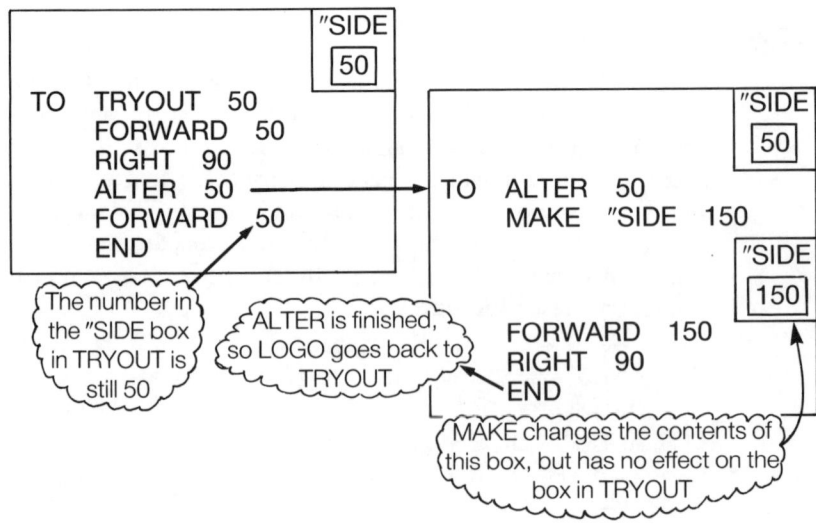

15.5 Levels

It would be nice to be able to draw POLYs in different colours without having to change the procedure each time. Here is how to do this; start by typing in these procedures:

```
TO   POLY  :SIDE  :ANGLE
     SETPC  :COLOUR
     REPEAT  (REPTS  :ANGLE)  [FORWARD  :SIDE  RIGHT
        :ANGLE]
     END

TO   REPTS  :ANGLE
     OP  (360  /  :ANGLE)
     END
```

When you run POLY, LOGO will complain that COLOUR has no value in POLY. And it is quite right to complain – you have not created the variable "COLOUR. You can mend this bug in one of two ways. First, you already know how to put the variable "COLOUR in the title line of a procedure:

> POLY :SIDE :ANGLE :COLOUR

This creates a "COLOUR box for POLY, and so makes "COLOUR a local variable in POLY. If you do this, you will have to type in a number for "COLOUR each time you run the procedure.

The second method is to create a box for "COLOUR, and put a value in it, direct from the keyboard. The number you put in the box stays there until you change it. You use MAKE to create this box; type:

> MAKE "COLOUR 3

This creates a *keyboard level* box:

> "COLOUR
> 3

We can think of procedures as being at *lower levels* than the keyboard. For example:

Level 0	Keyboard
Level 1	POLY
Level 2	REPTS

When you make a box labelled "COLOUR direct from the keyboard, it is a Level 0 box, and it can be borrowed by any procedures at lower levels which do not have their own "COLOUR boxes.
POLY :SIDE :ANGLE is a procedure at the next level down (Level 1). You call it from the keyboard by typing a command such as POLY 200 120. POLY itself calls the procedure REPTS, which works

out how many repetitions of a side of the polygon must be drawn. REPTS is at Level 2, because it is called by the Level 1 procedure POLY. The diagram shows what happens when you run these procedures.

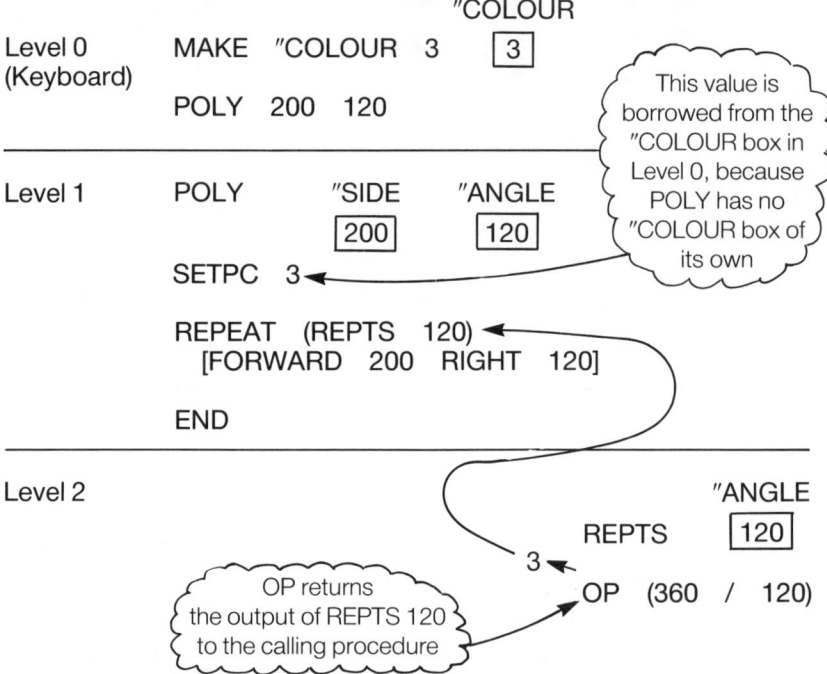

The box labelled "COLOUR, which you created at Level 0, can be used by every procedure in the workspace, because whenever a procedure is called, that procedure is below Level 0. The box "COLOUR at Level 0 is often called a *global variable*, because it can be borrowed by all Level 1 procedures, and by all the procedures which they call. Hence, all the procedures in the workspace can borrow a Level 0 variable; that is why it is called a global variable.

Now you have made a "COLOUR box and put the value 3 into it; the procedure

    POLY :SIDE :ANGLE

will run, and will draw using the colour 3.

Other procedures can make use of the value you have given to the global variable "COLOUR. Try

    TO SQCOL :SIDE
        SETPC :COLOUR
        REPEAT 4 [FORWARD :SIDE RIGHT 90]
        END

LOGO will not complain about this, because "COLOUR is at Level 0 and so is a global variable; it has the value 3. You can also make global variables from within procedures. Because LOGO can only create boxes for local variables when you write the names of the variables in the title line of a procedure, it follows that if you use MAKE to create a new variable within a procedure, the procedure does not have a box for it, and so LOGO makes a new box *at Level 0*. For example, if you do

```
TO   SQ   :SIDE
     MAKE   "SHADE   4
     SETPC   :SHADE
     REPEAT   4   [FORWARD   :SIDE   RIGHT   90]
     END
```

then "SHADE is a new name, so it becomes the name of a global variable and can be used by any procedure. When you have run SQ, type:

```
PRINT   :SHADE
PRINT   :SIDE
```

The variable "SHADE is a global variable and is accessible from the keyboard, so LOGO replies to PRINT :SHADE with 4. On the other hand, "SIDE is local to the procedure SQ, and Level 0 cannot look into the "SIDE box belonging to SQ, so LOGO complains that SIDE has no value. In fact, you have not created this variable at keyboard level – "SIDE is inside the procedure SQ, so it can never be accessible to a keyboard command to PRINT its value.

15.6 Changing colours

In many of your drawings, you must have wanted to change colours automatically within a procedure, so as to produce a multi-coloured effect. A POLYSPI would look very handsome if successive sides were in different colours. You can now arrange for this to happen – here is a possible colour changing procedure for MODE 2:

```
TO   CHCOL
     MAKE   "COL   (:COL   +   1)
     IF   (:COL   =   16)   [MAKE   "COL   1]
     SETPC   :COL
     END
```

This procedure will not run by itself. When you ask it to MAKE "COL (:COL + 1) it needs to know what number :COL represents, and as you have not told it, it complains. Thus, you must be sure to make a higher level "COL box, either by making it directly from the keyboard at Level 0, or you can make the "COLOUR box within a procedure which calls CHCOL. Here is one possibility:

```
TO  TRICOL  :SIDE
    MAKE  "COL  1
    REPEAT  3  [FORWARD  :SIDE  RIGHT  120  CHCOL]
END
```

The diagram shows the way CHCOL borrows from TRICOL if you type TRICOL 200.

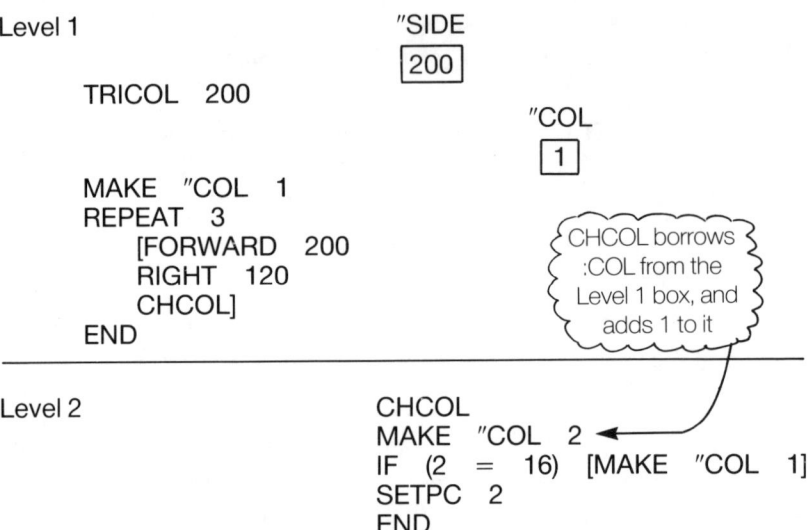

15.7 Project

Do some colour changes within drawings such as POLYSPI. You might also try random colour changes.

16 Building up lists

16.1 A random sentence generator

Projects of this type enable a learner to build up random sentences, and to see whether these sentences seem right; this may help the learner to focus on the grammatical features of writing. In this chapter we shall build a very simple procedure of this type. At each recursion, the computer asks you to teach it a noun and a verb, and it then makes a random sentence from the lists of nouns and verbs built up so far.

The basic structure is:

```
MESSAGE
NOUN
VERB
MAKESENT
MESSAGE
```

MESSAGE is a *superprocedure*; its only function is to call the procedures NOUN and VERB, which ask you to teach it words, and then the procedure MAKESENT, which makes and prints the random sentence. Recursion is then used to repeat the procedure MESSAGE, so that the lists of nouns and verbs grow every time MESSAGE is called.

The procedures NOUN and VERB use the command RL to obtain a word as input from the keyboard and store it temporarily as a list in "INP.

```
TO   NOUN
TYPE  [TEACH  ME  A  NOUN]
MAKE  "INP  RL
MAKE  "NOUNL  LPUT  FIRST  :INP  :NOUNL

TO   VERB
TYPE  [TEACH  ME  A  VERB]
MAKE  "INP  RL
MAKE  "VERBL  LPUT  FIRST  :INP  :VERBL
```

In order to run these procedures, you will need to create the boxes "NOUNL and "VERBL, and put empty lists in them. You can do this from the keyboard with:

```
        MAKE   "NOUNL   []
```
and   `MAKE   "VERBL   []`

16.2 LPUT and FPUT

The command LPUT has been used to add new words to the lists "NOUNL and "VERBL. The syntax is:

    LPUT   expression   list

The *expression* is added to the end of the *list* (Last PUT). Thus, if

    "NOUNL contains [DOGS CATS],

and [RABBITS] has been input to "INP, then

    MAKE   "NOUNL   LPUT   (FIRST   :INP)   :NOUNL

constructs the list

    [DOGS   CATS   RABBITS]

in "NOUNL. In this case, the *list* is the contents of "NOUNL, and the *expression* is FIRST :INP. It is necessary to use FIRST :INP, rather than just :INP, as the expression to be tacked on to the end of "NOUNL, because :INP is the list [RABBITS], and we only want the word "RABBITS to be added to the list.

There is another command, FPUT (First PUT), which can be used to add an expression at the *beginning* of a list. Its syntax is:

    FPUT   expression   list

In the procedures NOUN and VERB, it does not matter whether the new words which the child teaches the computer are tacked on at the beginning or the end of the lists of nouns and verbs, because the next move will be to select random words from the lists. In other programs, it may be extremely important at which end of a list a new expression is put.

16.3 Choosing a random member of a list

The following procedure chooses a random word from the list of words stored in the list "L. The word is returned as an output.

```
TO   RANDWD  :L
MAKE  "A  (COUNT  :L)  +  1
MAKE  "R  RANDOM  :A
IF  :R  =  0  [RANDWD  :L]
OP  ITEM  :R  :L
END
```

The primitive

    COUNT

counts the number of elements in a list, or the number of letters in a word. RANDOM chooses a random whole number in the range from 0 up to one less than the number which is its input. We then have to pick out the chosen element of the list. The primitive

  ITEM number list

then picks out the designated element of the list :L.

16.4 Making the random sentence

To build the random sentence, we choose a random word from "NOUNL and a random word from "VERBL, enclose each one in a list, and then join the two lists together into a single list by using the primitive SE (stands for SEntence), as follows:

```
TO   MAKESENT
     MAKE  "SUBJ  RANDWD  :NOUNL
     MAKE  "VERB  RANDWD  :VERBL
     MAKE  "SENT  (SE  "THE  :SUBJ  :VERB)
     PRINT :SENT
```

Now the procedure MESSAGE, given in paragraph 16.1, can be used to put together the sub-procedures into the complete program.

You can improve the appearance of MAKESENT on the screen in several ways. A blank line can be printed after each sentence by using

  PRINT "

which prints an empty line. You can achieve a space after the screen display

  TEACH ME A NOUN

by writing

  TYPE [TEACH ME A NOUN \ ]

The backslash \ tells LOGO to treat the next character to which it comes literally; in this case, when the next character is a space, LOGO prints a space rather than ignoring the space.

A superprocedure, WRITER, can be used to avoid the need to create "NOUNL and "VERBL at the keyboard at the start of a session:

```
TO   WRITER
     MAKE  "NOUNL  [ ]
     MAKE  "VERBL  [ ]
     MESSAGE
     END
```

16.5 Projects

1. Improve MESSAGE. You might want longer sentences, or you might want a facility for the user to view and change the word lists. You might want to avoid having to teach the computer new words at every round.

2. Write some (pseudo-Japanese) Haiku poetry using random choices from word lists. A Haiku poem has three lines, and a structure like that of the following example:

   LATE COOL SHOWERS FALL.
   TINY BLOSSOMS OPEN AND
   GREET THE NEW WARM SUN.

   The structure is:

   adjective adjective noun verb.
   adjective noun verb *and*
   verb *the* adjective adjective noun.

   Haiku poems are always about nature and its beauties, so you will need lists of appropriate nouns, adjectives and verbs to go in each place in the poem.

   You could also work out how many different Haiku poems could be made from the word lists with which you have supplied LOGO.

17 More about recursion

17.1 Drawing a tree

A very simple procedure draws two branches of a tree, and finishes with the Turtle facing the way it started.

```
TO   VEE  :LENGTH
    LEFT  45
    FORWARD   :LENGTH
    BACK  :LENGTH
    RIGHT  90
    FORWARD   :LENGTH
    BACK  :LENGTH
    LEFT  45
    END
```

We can make a tree by drawing a smaller VEE at the tip of each branch, and continuing to do this recursively.

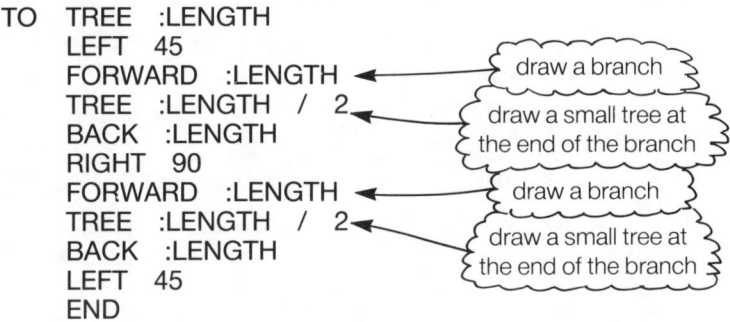

Unfortunately, this gets bogged down in the left-hand branch, and never ends until the computer runs out of memory. To see why, look at the drawing of TREE 16 below:

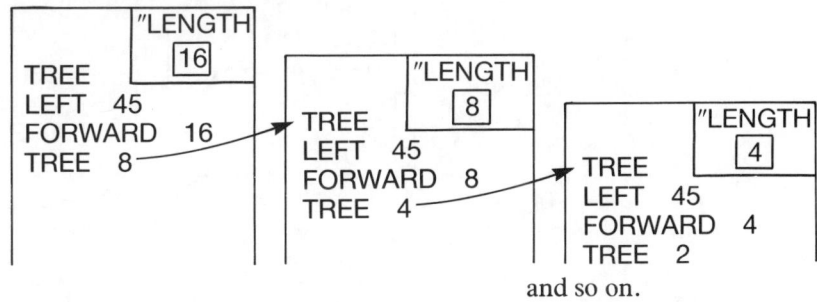

and so on.

We need to stop drawing smaller trees at an appropriate point when the branches are short. Put in the *stop line*

```
IF  :LENGTH  <  8  [STOP]
```

right after the title, so that you have

```
TO   TREE  :LENGTH
     IF  :LENGTH  <  8  [STOP]
     LEFT  45
     FORWARD  :LENGTH
     TREE  :LENGTH  /  2
     BACK  :LENGTH
     RIGHT  90
     FORWARD  :LENGTH
     TREE  :LENGTH  /  2
     BACK  :LENGTH
     LEFT  45
     END
```

The best place to put a stop line in recursion is usually immediately after the title. Notice that the command STOP stops execution of the procedure in which it occurs, and returns control to the procedure which called it. If you ever want to stop completely and return control to the keyboard, use TOPLEVEL.

After this change, the whole tree miraculously draws itself. Follow a small TREE to see why:

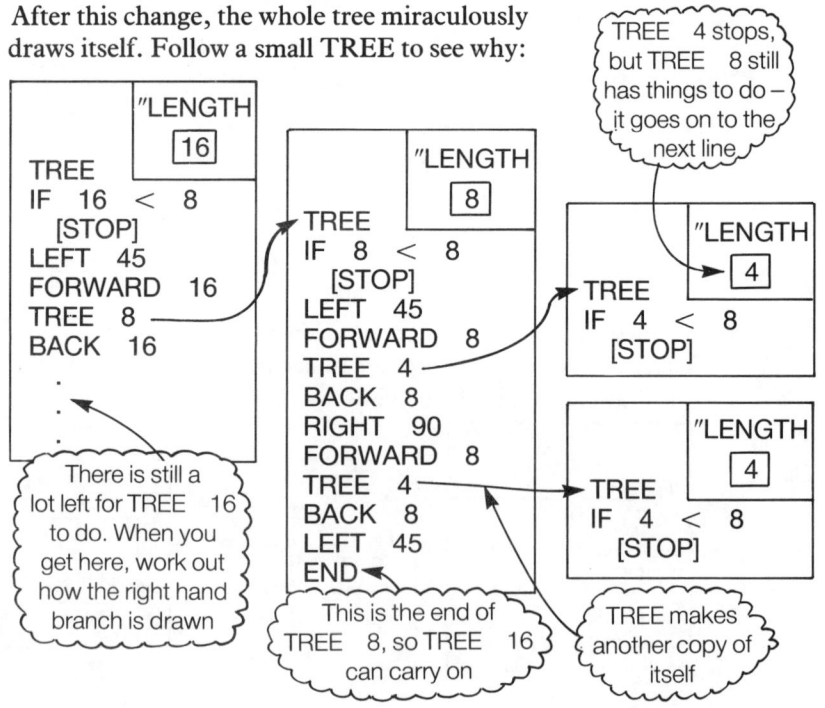

LOGO has some facilities for tracing the progress of your programs, which may help you to follow what is going on in recursion. Type

>   TRACE

before running a procedure, and LOGO will print the name of the procedure it is executing, and the values of the variables used, each time it starts on a new procedure. To turn the TRACE facility off, simply type TRACE again. However, it may all happen too fast for you to take it in. In this case, incorporate the command

>   WAIT   number

into the procedure; you choose the number according to the number of *sixtieths of a second* that you want LOGO to wait before doing the next command; thus, WAIT 30 produces a half-second pause before the next command.

17.2 Variations on TREE

You can make one branch of VEE longer than the other. You can vary the angle between branches (you can use a variable to do this).

You can use different stop rules. The next one uses the variable DEPTH – each branch grows a tree of depth one less.

```
TO   TREE  1  :LENGTH   :DEPTH
     IF  :DEPTH  =  0  [STOP]
     LEFT  45
     FORWARD   :LENGTH
     TREE1  :LENGTH  /  2  :DEPTH  -  1
     BACK  :LENGTH
     RIGHT  90
     FORWARD   :LENGTH
     TREE1  :LENGTH  /  2  :DEPTH  -  1
     BACK  :LENGTH
     LEFT  45
     END
```

17.3 Snowflake curves

A snowflake curve, as well as being very beautiful, has the strange mathematical property that if it could be drawn completely if would be of infinite length, while fitting in to the area of a basic hexagon which encloses the snowflake. Of course the computer cannot actually draw a curve of infinite length, but LOGO can enable us to draw a good enough approximation to see how it would ideally work, and so help us to visualise a curve of infinite length fitting in to a finite area. Curves of this type were discovered late in the nineteenth century, and for some time they were regarded as tiresome mathematical paradoxes. Drawing curves of this type, and working out the lengths of their perimeters, may enable you to realise how the perimeter of a shape may be greatly increased without making much difference to the area. This concept is usually found difficult by many people, who have little experience which would enable them to form the idea.

We start building the snowflake by drawing an equilateral triangle of convenient size; a good length for each side is either 243 or 486 Turtle steps, because we are going to do a lot of dividing by 3.

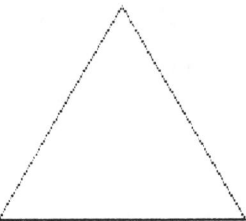

The method of building the snowflake is to replace the middle third of each side by a 'tooth' which sticks out from the side:

This produces a new shape, which looks like this:

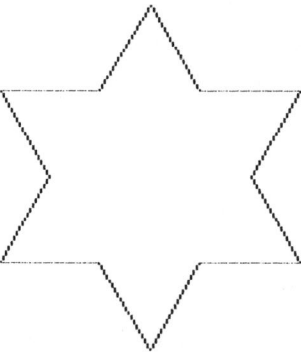

It has a greater perimeter – putting the 'tooth' on each side increases the length of that side by one-third. In the example above, the middle third of the line was of length 27 turtle steps, and has been replaced by two lines of length 27 turtle steps. Thus, the length of the line has been multiplied by 4/3.

The snowflake curve is drawn by continuing to do this – whenever we see a line, we replace the middle third of it by a 'tooth'. The next step is shown in the following diagram:

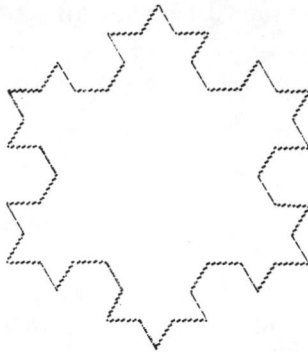

We could, in theory, go on doing this for ever, and recursion is an appropriate way of programming it. However, in practice a stopping method is needed; we shall stop when the size of a 'tooth' is less than a limiting short length such as 1 unit.

The basic pattern for drawing a tooth is:

```
TO   TOOTH   :LENGTH
     FORWARD   :LENGTH  /  3
     LEFT  60
     FORWARD   :LENGTH  /  3
     RIGHT  120
     FORWARD   :LENGTH  /  3
     LEFT  60
     FORWARD   :LENGTH  /  3
     END
```

This gives the basis for a recursive procedure to draw a side of the snowflake like this:

```
TO   SIDE   :LENGTH   :LIM
     IF  :LENGTH  <  :LIM  [FORWARD  :LENGTH  STOP]
     SIDE   :LENGTH  /  3   :LIM
     LEFT  60
     SIDE   :LENGTH  /  3   :LIM
     RIGHT  120
     SIDE   :LENGTH  /  3   :LIM
     LEFT  60
     SIDE   :LENGTH  /  3   :LIM
     END
```

The whole snowflake can now be drawn:

```
TO   SNOWFLAKE   :LENGTH   :LIM
     SIDE   :LENGTH   :LIM
     RIGHT  120
     SNOWFLAKE   :LENGTH   :LIM
     END
```

You should experiment with snowflakes with different stopping conditions, such as:

```
SNOWFLAKE   243   27
SNOWFLAKE   243   9
SNOWFLAKE   243   3
SNOWFLAKE   243   1
```

17.4 Project

The C-curve is another recursively drawn curve. The idea here is to replace a line by an 'elbow' consisting of two lines drawn at right angles.

The basic procedure to replace a line of given length by an 'elbow' is:

```
TO  ELBOW  :LENGTH
    LEFT  45
    FORWARD  :LENGTH  /  SQRT  2
    RIGHT  90
    FORWARD  :LENGTH  /  SQRT  2
    LEFT  45
    END
```

Incorporate this into a recursive procedure with a stop when :LENGTH < :LIMIT. A possible method is shown below:

```
TO  ELBOW  :LENGTH  :LIM
    IF  :LENGTH  <  :LIM  [FORWARD  :LENGTH  STOP]
    LEFT  45
    ELBOW  :LENGTH  /  SQRT  2  :LIM
    RIGHT  90
    ELBOW  :LENGTH  /  SQRT  2  :LIM
    LEFT  45
    END
```

The 'Dragon' curve is a similar curve, which has elbows pointing alternately on the two sides of the previous line. Experiment with this.

18 List of LOGO primitives

In this chapter are listed in groups (not in alphabetical order) the LOGO primitives used in this manual. These primitives are the greater part of the complete set of BBC LOGO primitives. A complete list will be found in the *BBC LOGO manual*. The section number beside each primitive indicates the first section where that primitive is described.

The commands are classified in groups according to their function, so as to aid retrieval.

Graphics commands

FORWARD (abbr. FD)	1.1
BACK (abbr. BK)	1.1
LEFT (abbr. LT)	1.1
RIGHT (abbr. RT)	1.1
HOME	1.1
CS (stands for ClearScreen)	1.1
CLEAN	1.1
PD (stands for PenDown)	1.2
PU (stands for PenUp)	1.2
SETPC	5.5
SETBG	5.5
WRAP	2.6
FENCE	2.6
WINDOW	2.6
SETX (stands for SET X-coordinate)	8.7
SETY (stands for SET Y-coordinate)	8.7
SETPOS (stands for SET POSition)	8.7
SETH (stands for SET Heading)	7.3
ST (stands for ShowTurtle)	5.1
HT (stands for HideTurtle)	5.1
CT (stands for ClearText)	5.2
TS (stands for TextScreen)	5.2
MODE	5.4
SETMODE	5.4

Numerical Commands

+	9.3
−	9.3
*	9.3
/	9.3
SUM	10.4

PROD (stands for PRODuct)	10.4
DIV (stands for DIVide)	10.4
QUOT (stands for QUOTient)	10.3
REMAINDER	10.3
INT (stands for INTeger part)	10.2
ROUND	10.2
SQRT (stands for SQuare RooT)	10.2
RANDOM	10.1

Building Procedures

TO	3.1
EDIT	4.1
function keys	4.5
EDALL (stands for EDit ALL procedures)	4.4
ERASE (abbr. ER)	3.3
ERALL (stands for ERase ALL)	4.6

Debugging

TRACE	17.1
WAIT	17.1

Words and Lists

FIRST	12.2
BF (stands for ButFirst)	12.2
LAST	12.5
BL (stands for ButLast)	12.5
LIST	12.5
SE (stands for SEntence)	12.5
ASCII	13.2
FPUT (stands for First PUT)	16.2
LPUT (stands for Last PUT)	16.2
COUNT	16.3
ITEM	16.3

Conditionals and tests

IF	10.6
<, >	10.6
=	10.6
LIST?	11.6
WORD?	11.6
NUMBER?	11.6
KEY?	13.4
EMPTY?	14.3
EQUAL?	14.3
MEMBER?	14.3
NOT	14.1
AND	14.2
OR	14.2

Control

STOP	17.1
TOPLEVEL	17.1
OP (stands for OutPut)	9.5
REPEAT	2.3

User Input and Output

PRINT (abbr. PR)	9.4
TYPE	11.8
SHOW	11.4
RL (stands for ReadList)	11.2
RC (stands for ReadCharacter)	13.1
SETCURSOR	11.8
\(backslash)	16.4

Variables

MAKE	9.1

Information and Files

POALL (stands for PrintOut ALL)	5.3
SAVE	3.5
SAVEALL	5.3
LOAD	3.5
OPPS (stands for OutPut ProcedureS)	5.3

Glossary

This glossary lists differences between Logotron LOGO for the BBC Micro and some other dialects of LOGO. It should enable you to use this book if you have a different version of LOGO. You will see that all dialects of LOGO contain many of the same commands, although the words used are sometimes different. You should also refer to the manual which came with your own version of LOGO, especially to find out details of how to build and edit procedures.

Many of the differences between different dialects of LOGO centre on the use of the *quotes* which indicate a *name*. RML LOGO for the 380Z/480Z uses a single quotation mark ', while the other dialects use a double quotation mark ". In the glossary, examples are used to show where you should use quotation marks.

The symbols n, w and l are used in the glossary to show the type of input which a command takes:

    n stands for the input of a *number*
    w stands for the input of a *word*
    l stands for the input of a *list*
    e stands for the input of an *expression* (number, word or list)

Abbreviated forms of the commands are given in brackets e.g. (FD)

Graphics commands

Logotron LOGO for the BBC	Spectrum LOGO	Apple LOGO	Terrapin LOGO for the Apple	380Z/480Z LOGO
FORWARD (FD) n	FORWARD (FD) n	FORWARD (FD) n	FORWARD (FD) n	FORWARD (FD) n
BACK (BK) n	BACK (BK) n	BACK (BK) n	BACK (BK) n	BACKWARD (BD) n
LEFT (LT) n	LEFT (LT) n	LEFT (LT) n	LEFT (LT) n	LEFT (LT) n
RIGHT (RT) n	RIGHT (RT) n	RIGHT (RT) n	RIGHT (RT) n	RIGHT (RT) n
HOME	HOME	HOME	HOME	CENTRE (CT)
			DRAW	–
CS	CLEARSCREEN (CS)	CLEARSCREEN (CS)	CLEARSCREEN (CS)	CLEAN (CL)
CLEAN	CLEAN	CLEAN		

PD	PENDOWN (PD)	PENDOWN (PD)	PENDOWN (PD)	PENCIL n
PU	PENUP (PU)	PENUP (PU)	PENUP (PU)	LIFT
SETPC n	SETPC n	SETPC n	PENCOLOR (PC) n	PENCIL n
SETBG n	SETBG n	SETBG n	BACKGROUND (BG) n	–
WRAP	WRAP	WRAP	WRAP	EDGES
FENCE	FENCE	FENCE	FENCE	NOEDGES
WINDOW	WINDOW	WINDOW	NOWRAP	–
SETX n	SETX n	SETX n	SETX n	SETX n
SETY n	SETY n	SETY n	SETY n	SETY n
SETPOS [n n]	SETPOS [n n]	SETPOS [n n]	SETXY n n	–
SETH n	SETH n	SETH n	SETH n	SETH n
ST	SHOWTURTLE (ST)	SHOWTURTLE (ST)	SHOWTURTLE (ST)	REVEAL
HT	HIDETURTLE (HT)	HIDETURTLE (HT)	HIDETURTLE (HT)	HIDE
CT	CT	CLEARTEXT	CLEARTEXT	–
TS	TEXTSCREEN (TS)	TEXTSCREEN	NODRAW	TEXT
(Use CS)	–	SPLITSCREEN	SPLITSCREEN	MIX
(Use CT)	–	FULLSCREEN	FULLSCREEN	DRAWING
MODE	–	–	–	–
SETMODE	–	–	–	–

Numerical Commands

+	+	+	+	ADD n n
–	–	–	–	SUBTRACT n n
*	*	*	*	MULTIPLY n n
/	/	/	/	DIVIDE n n
SUM n n	SUM n n	SUM n n		
–	–	–		
PROD n n	PRODUCT n n	PRODUCT n n		
DIV n n	DIV n n	–		

+, –, *, / are only available in newer versions of 380Z/480Z LOGO. Otherwise, use the prefix commands below.

QUOT n n	REMAINDER n n	QUOTIENT n n	QUOTIENT n n	QUOTIENT n n	SHARE n n
REMAINDER n n	INT n	REMAINDER n n	REMAINDER n n	REMAINDER n n	REMAINDER n n
INT n	ROUND n	INT n	INTEGER n	–	–
ROUND n	SQRT n	ROUND n	ROUND n	–	–
SQRT n	RANDOM n	SQRT n	SQRT n	–	SQT n
RANDOM n	–	RANDOM n	RANDOM n	–	PICK n
–		–	–		RANDOM

Building Procedures

Many of the differences between dialects of LOGO occur in building procedures; examples of the use of these commands in building and editing the procedure SQUARE are shown. Take care to be precise in the use of *quotes*.

TO SQUARE	TO SQUARE	TO "SQUARE	TO SQUARE	TO SQUARE	BUILD 'SQUARE
EDIT "SQUARE	EDIT "SQUARE	EDIT "SQUARE	EDIT SQUARE		CHANGE 'SQUARE
EDALL	–	–			
ERASE "SQUARE	ERASE "SQUARE	ERASE "SQUARE	ERASE SQUARE		SCRAP 'SQUARE
ERALL	ERALL	ERPS	ERASE ALL		–

Procedures with variables

An example is given below; it takes two inputs, draws a line and turns through an angle. Note the use of *quotes* and *colons* in the different dialects of LOGO.

TO BIT :L :A	TO BIT :L :A	TO BIT :L :A	TO BIT :L :A	TO BIT :L :A	BUILD BIT 'L 'A
FORWARD :L	FORWARD :L	FORWARD :L	FORWARD :L	FORWARD :L	FORWARD :L
RIGHT :A	RIGHT :A	RIGHT :A	RIGHT :A	RIGHT :A	RIGHT :A
END	END	END	END	END	

Words and Lists

FIRST e	FIRST e	FIRST e	FIRST e	FIRST e	FIRST wl
BF e	BUTFIRST (BF) e	BUTFIRST (BF) e	BUTFIRST (BF) e	BUTFIRST (BF) e	REST wl

LAST e	LAST e	LAST e	—
BL e	BUTLAST (BL) e	BUTLAST (BL) e	—
LIST e e	LIST e e	LIST e e	—
SE e e	SENTENCE (SE) e e	SENTENCE (SE) e e	JOIN l l
ASCII char	ASCII char	ASCII char	
FPUT e l	FPUT e l	FPUT e l	PUTFIRST e l
LPUT e l	LPUT e l	LPUT e l	PUTLAST l e
COUNT e	COUNT l	—	—
ITEM n l	ITEM n l	—	l # n

Conditionals and control

Note the differences in syntax in different dialects; an example is given of the use of IF.

IF :X = 0	IF :X = 0	IF :X = 0	IF :X = 0
[FD 30] [RT 90]	[FD 30] [RT 90]	THEN FD 30	THEN FD 30
		ELSE RT 90	ELSE RT 90
n < n	n < n	n < n	LESSQ (LSQ) n n
n > n	n > n	n > n	GREATERQ (GRQ) n n
e = e	e = e	e = e	EQUALQ (EQQ) e e
LIST? e	LISTP e	LIST? e	LISTQ (LQ) e
WORD? e	WORDP e	WORD? e	WORDQ (WQ) e
NUMBER? e	NUMBERP e	NUMBER? e	NUMBERQ (NQ) e
KEY?	KEYP	RC?	KEYQ
EMPTY? e	EMPTYP e	—	EMPTYQ (EMQ) e
EQUAL? e e	EQUALP e e	—	EQUALQ (EQQ) e e
MEMBER? e l	MEMBERP e l	—	—
NOT	NOT	NOT	NOT
AND	AND	ALLOF	BOTH
OR	OR	ANYOF	EITHER
STOP	STOP	STOP	STOP

TOPLEVEL	TOPLEVEL	THROW "TOPLEVEL	TOPLEVEL	
OP	OUTPUT (OP)	OUTPUT (OP)	OUTPUT (OP)	RESULT
REPEAT n l	REPEAT n l	REPEAT n l	REPEAT n l	

User Input and Output

PRINT (PR)	PRINT (PR)	PRINT (PR)	PRINT (PR)	PRINT
TYPE	TYPE	TYPE	PRINT1	
SHOW	SHOW	SHOW		SAY
RL	READLIST (RL)	READLIST (RL)	REQUEST (RQ)	ASK
RC	READCHAR (RC)	READCHAR (RC)	READCHARACTER (RC)	KEY
SETCURSOR [n n]	SETCURSOR [n n]	SETCURSOR [n n]	CURSOR [n n]	
(SETCUR)				

Variables

An example of the use of MAKE is given:
MAKE "SIDE 40   MAKE "SIDE 40   MAKE "SIDE 40   MAKE "SIDE 40   MAKE 'SIDE 40

Information and Files

POALL	POALL	POALL	PRINTOUT ALL	
SAVE	SAVE	SAVE	SAVE	KEEP (consult manual)
SAVEALL	SAVEALL	SAVEALL		
LOAD	LOAD	LOAD	READ	GET
OPPS	POTS	POTS	POTS	INDEX